Sensible Grace

Visual Tools for a Better Life

Dr. Mark Wickstrom

Sensible Grace

ISBN: 978-0-9961137-0-0

Author: Dr. Mark Wickstrom

Requests for permission or further information should be addressed to the publisher.

Publisher: MDW Press
2524 Furnace Creek Ave.
Henderson, NV. 89074

MDWPress@gmail.com

The author may be contacted at the following address:
MDW Press, LLC
2524 Furnace Creek Ave.
Henderson, NV 89074

To order additional copies of this title, email MDWPress@gmail.com or visit www.MDWPress.com

Printed in the United States of America

DEDICATION

To all the people who invited me to help them
explore their perplexing life situations.
Their willingness to be open and honest allowed me the
opportunity to discover, adapt and utilize these diagrams
to help bring insight and understanding to their life.

Jen —
I hope the tools prove to be
as helpful to you as they have been
for me! God bless

TABLE OF CONTENTS

Introduction

1 Parent, Adult, Child   1
   Understanding how we interact with others

2 The Awareness Wheel   15
   Clarifying issues with others

3 The Karpman Drama Triangle   29
   How to help others without getting hurt

4 Interdependence   45
   How to fall in love and stay in love

5 Landing Lights   55
   Assessing changes in your life

6 The Block System   63
   Maintaining balance in work and life

7 Levels of Communication   75
   Choosing the style that will serve you best

8 Healthy Grief   87
   Discovering the good that can come from a difficult situation

9 Parent, Adult, Child Case Studies   95
   Practice in using PAC

10 Awareness Wheel Case Studies   105
    Practice in using The Awareness Wheel

11 Exercises in Building Interdependence   115
    Additional Exercises in Interdependence

    Bibliography   123

    About the Author   124

ACKNOWLEDGMENTS

I am grateful to the authors who created the individual diagrams.

I am grateful to Jennifer Allen for creating the graphics used in this book.

I am grateful to Brenda Prinzavalli for patiently teaching me the intricacies of computer publishing.

I am grateful to Kelli Andino for assistance for creating the logo design.

I am grateful to Carol Anderson for reading and giving feedback on the book.

I am grateful to Blaire Wickstrom, my daughter, who edited the book.

I am grateful to Kristi Wickstrom, my wife, who gave honest feedback on the contents of the book.

Introduction

As a pastor I talk about God's grace quite frequently. Grace is the unmerited favor that is available because of God's unconditional love, Jesus' amazing forgiveness and the presence of the Holy Spirit to lead us and guide us in all things spiritual. So often "grace" is seen in only its eternal form. God's grace provides eternal life to those who accept this divine gift.

Sensible Grace, on the other hand, is the grace that comes to us in the form of an insight or "aha" moment when we see a circumstance, situation or relationship in a whole new light. It brings us a sense of relief. An imaginary weight has been lifted. A burden has been taken away. For this insight to happen we often need a catalyst. It may come in the form of a comment from another person, or it may come from doing some analysis on our own.

I am a visual person. I tend to do my best thinking and processing when I can put a situation into some tangible form on a white board, a piece of paper or more recently on the notes section of my cell phone or iPad.

Over the decades of doing ministry with people of all ages, I have had the pleasure of discovering a series of diagrams that have consistently assisted me in helping people see complicated situations in new and clearer light.

To give you an example, a woman came into my office and said, "I have never come to a pastor before today." It was a refreshingly honest confession. I had to admit I wondered what issue she was pondering that got her to pick up the phone and make such an unusual call. It didn't take her long to pour out the hurt in her life. Her second husband had recently died after a long, difficult illness. During the illness he had transformed from the kind, thoughtful man she had married into a demanding, demeaning impatient patient. Intellectually she knew it was the combination of terminal illness and chemical treatments that transformed his outlook and actions. However, she was having a hard time resolving the conflicting feelings of relief and guilt that she felt after he died. Her feeling of relief came from the reality that his painful journey was over. Her relief was also tied to knowing she no longer had to care for his every need. Her feelings of guilt, however, stemmed from the feelings of gladness that he was gone and that his abusive demands had come to an end.

Over the course of the session, I used a couple of the diagrams you are about to discover. As I shared the diagram on grieving she commented that it was helping her understand the emotional journey she was on. As we talked about the Karpman drama triangle diagram, she recognized the source of her resentment toward her husband during those last unpleasant months of his and her ordeal. I handed her the piece of paper I had drawn each of the diagrams on, and I encouraged her to put the yellow sheet on her refrigerator door. "A visual reminder of where you have been and how you can consider moving ahead," I told her. As we finished our conversation she thanked me for the insights. She smiled at me, and I could see and sense the relief in her demeanor.

It was at that moment that the title for this book became clear to me. I told this grieving widow that I was offering her God's sensible grace. She had come into my office feeling weighed down and uncomfortable about the mixture of emotions that surrounded her husband's illness and death. But after the conversation, she was feeling relief. The burdens had been lifted and she was set free from the guilt and confusion.

Each of the diagrams mentioned in this book has had just such a liberating experience for people I've shared them with over the years.

God's sensible grace frees a person up from misunderstanding, confusion, even emotional turmoil. Sensible grace is meant to be used in this life, to provide insight and relief here and now. It is an unmerited favor of insight on a circumstance or situation.

My encouragement is that as you read about each of these diagrams you will see them as tools. Like any tool, they can be applied to countless situations. Please keep in mind that when a tool is applied properly to a situation, every task is made infinitely easier. I hope your emotional, psychological "tool box" will be enriched by the diagrams described in this book. As you seek to apply these tools to your life circumstances I am hopeful that you will discover the same kind of insight and relief that my parishioners, friends, and family members have discovered over the years.

CHAPTER 1
PARENT, ADULT, CHILD
UNDERSTANDING HOW WE
INTERACT WITH OTHERS

In 1967 Dr. Thomas Harris wrote a best-selling book *I'm Ok, You're Ok*. It helped launch the movement in psychology known as "transactional analysis". Dr. Harris was able to integrate the work of Doctor Eric Berne and Doctor Wilder Penfield into a new way to analyze how people interact. This book became a resource I have used almost every week and sometimes multiple times a day as I help people understand how they interact with one another.

For example, one afternoon a parishioner came to see me. She had set the appointment because she was troubled about her relationship with her grown daughter. I invited her to give me an example of how they interacted. She proceeded to describe a recent conversation that had deteriorated into a verbal altercation between the two. I grabbed a piece of paper and drew two rectangles (in the shape of a traffic light) each with three circles in them.

"Each of you is made up of three component circles I call tapes" I started. "The bottom circle is called the Child,…and it is the spontaneous, creative, fun loving, selfish and irresponsible parts of you. No one had to teach you to be selfish. In fact, we all start life, and we cry when we want food, fuss when we want attention, fill our diapers spontaneously and think nothing of it. We made noises as we pleased."

"At the same time we are expressing ourselves so freely in the child tape, we are constantly receiving feedback from our environment. This feedback accumulates in the brain, and we begin creating the top circle or what I call the Parent tape. These tapes are characterized as all of the should do, ought to do, must do, don't ever do messages that are programed into us by the age of six. Obviously, a child has no control over who contributes to the parent tapes. It can be parents, siblings, neighbors, relatives, teachers, coaches, pastors, even strangers who enter a child's life at any given point in those first six years. The circle of Parent tapes never go away. They will always be there as a voice reminding us of what we were instructed to do and not do.

The circle in the middle is called the Adult tape, and it begins to function somewhere around the tenth month of life. If the circle receives attention and encouragement, it will continue to grow throughout our lives. The Adult tape is able to constantly draw from the spontaneous messages of the Child tape and hear the Parent tape messages on the same subject. If nurtured, the Adult tape can help a person make the best decision for the situation. Let me give you an example of how the three work together.

As a pastor I have different style worship services in my church. There have been many occasions when the Child tape in me gets excited by the music we are singing and I have an urge to just yell out an "Amen!" The Parent tape instilled in me from my youth reminds me to be quiet in church. So the Adult tape hears the Child tape spontaneity and energy but also hears the Parent tape reservations about making unpredictable noises in church. The Adult tape can then ask the question: which service are you in, Mark? In our more traditional service the unexpected shout might be met with glares of Parent tape disapproval from other members who share that same tape. On the other hand, in our rock n roll service, the spontaneous shout would not be unwelcome at all;…in fact, it might be merely a part of a chorus of shouts from other folks in the congregation. The Adult tape enables me to decide which avenue of action I should pursue.

On paper I had drawn the two rectangles, one for the mother and the other for the adult daughter. I invited the mom to reflect on the conversation. Now, I suggested, determine which voice were you speaking from and how did your daughter hear that voice and respond.

The mother identified that she had definitely come out of the Parent tape telling her daughter "you should" act in a certain way. This Parental command was heard in the Child tape of the daughter, and the Child in her responded, "I am old enough to make my own decision about this matter". The Parent vs. Child conversation was neither helpful nor productive for either of them.

I invited the mom to rethink the conversation so that it took place in the Adult. The mom thought for a while and said that, she wasn't even sure how to do that. She was so accustomed to speaking to her daughter from the Parent that she didn't know how to converse in the Adult. I suggested that was part of the reason that the two were in conflict so often. The daughter was a grown-up who wanted to be treated like an adult and not talked to like a child.

As we reframed the conversation in the Adult version of the interaction, mom began to appreciate the importance of speaking from the Adult. However, we all find ourselves speaking from different circles at any given time. We also process what we hear from others in one of the three circles. Let's take a look at how those interpersonal conversations can be handled.

Parent> Child Interaction

This form of interaction can serve two different ends: helpful or harmful. Let's consider the helpful end first.

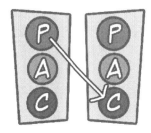

Helpful Parent>Child interactions are those that prepare kids for life. Learning how to walk and talk are times parent voices give lots of encouragement: "Way to go, you can do it. Go ahead try it again". Teaching children limits and boundaries: "don't touch the hot plate, you will get hurt!" "Don't cross the street without looking both ways" are wonderful gifts the parent voice provides the growing child. Teaching children manners: "what do you say to the nice man who gave you the cookie?" "Thank you". Training youngsters on etiquette, for example; which fork to use at a formal dinner party (outside one for the salad, largest fork for the main course); how to introduce a friend to an adult "Mr. Smith this is my friend Monica. Monica, this is my neighbor Mr. Smith". Helpful Parent>Child interactions also provide guidelines for future decision making. "Whenever you are going to bake a cake, be sure to grease the pan first". Such helpful tidbits of information give children skill sets that will enhance their interaction with the world the rest of their lives.

Harmful Parent>Child interactions are characterized by negative messages that can go on being played. I watched and listened as a mother and child interacted at a local grocery store one Saturday morning. "What do you mean you couldn't find the jelly? What are you, an idiot?" When the young man came back to their cart a few minutes later the woman's response was, "Way to go Einstein, you finally figured it out." If that child grows up in an environment where he is regularly demeaned, called names and generally spoken down to…his parent tape will inform him that that is how he should perceive himself and probably even how he should talk to others. On one hand he has all the potential of becoming a bully to peers and maybe even a bully to people of authority as well. On the other hand, he may be so filled with negative messages that he will underachieve the rest of his life. The parent>child interaction that is consistently critical in the early years can cause self-doubt. The child who was told he/she was stupid may not try new ventures in life because the parent tape is still screaming in his/her head that he/she is too dumb to succeed.

Child>Parent Interaction

This form of dialogue also has helpful and harmful ways of interacting.

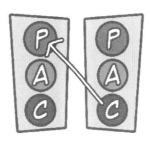

Helpful Child>Parent exchange would empower the child to help a person try new things. I recall touring the beautiful island of New Zealand with a group from my church. When we arrived in Queenstown I noticed an advertisement for XLR8 (a skydiving company). The child tape in me went wild. I've always wanted to jump out of a plane. Why, you may ask? Years ago I had a friend tell me, "When you jump out of a plane, you don't feel like you are falling." How could that be, I wondered. The parent tape in me was very apprehensive. Skydiving appears to be a dangerous activity. The parent tape wondered about how expensive it would be and how reliable are the pilots and veteran jump masters. The child tape in me said, "Let's do this!" The parent tape was hesitant and repeating the caution…"it may be too dangerous".

Fortunately, for me, the adult tape got involved, and after I had checked the price (reasonable) and the safety record (no one had ever been lost), the child circle won. As the plane took off the child tape excitement was wonderful. As we approached our jump altitude of 12,000 feet, the child tape was ecstatic, the parent tape nervous and the adult ready to follow all the safety instructions. When the jump master asked for the first volunteer to exit the plane my child tape shot up my hand. I didn't want to wait…let's do this! On the count of three I spread my arms and legs and felt my body move away from the plane. I was hurtling through space at 120 miles per hour, and I was enjoying a magnificent view of the mountains of the South Island. With the wind distorting my face, my goggles keeping my eyes open and clear, it felt more like riding a motorcycle really fast except without any noise and an amazing aerial view. It didn't feel like falling at all! The child tape had won and I was energized by the experience. Once the jump master opened the chute and we floated to our landing site I was impressed at how precisely we could steer and eventually land. The child tape had afforded me an experience that my parent tape would have easily put a kibosh on if the child tape hadn't been so persuasive. The child tape is often the risk taker, the part of us willing to try new and different things. When there is a positive experience gained, the child >parent dialogue can allow us new and different experiences.

The harmful Child>Parent dialogue is when the child continues to rule a person to the risk and endangerment of him or herself or others. I happen to believe that people who are suffering from the disease of chemical dependency are being controlled by their child tapes. The chemical abuser will choose his/her chemical of choice regardless of the pain it causes themselves, their loved ones and those they encounter. Countless lives have been damaged because the abuser wants what he/she wants, when he/she wants it, how he/she wants it, and it doesn't matter what negative consequences are created by the choice. An attitude of "Me first" is the mantra of the child driven adult. When the child tape is dominating a person or relationship there is seldom any logic involved in decision making.

As a young pastor I spent some time at the Johnson Institute in Minneapolis learning about the disease of chemical dependency. The institute shared one saying that stuck with me: "You cannot have a logical conversation with an illogical person." That is a perfect summation of what it is like to converse with an out of control child of any age.

I watched a grandfather try to have a logical conversation with an illogical six year old in a drug store. There was no convincing this very spoiled child of anything. Life was going to go the child's way period.

If he didn't get his way, the arm waving, leg kicking, voice shrieking tantrum would win the day. Adults who are consistently driven by their child tapes are often self-absorbed and their relationships suffer.

Child > Child Interaction

When the child tape in each person expresses its desires a power struggle is often a result. The example I like to use with couples goes like this. Imagine one of you gets an unexpected windfall bonus from work. One partner says "let's use the money to buy a Corvette". The other person says "Let's use the money to buy all new furniture for the house".

"You can't drive furniture"

"You can't fit anything in a Corvette".

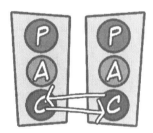

Each person has stated his/her desire…how will they decide which person's desire is fulfilled? When both people want their own way it is typically a meeting of the two child tapes. If the folks are not mature enough to go to the adult sphere for a resolution, the two child tapes will potentially argue until some form of power struggle resolves the issue.

Parent>Parent

The parent to parent conversation often sounds like two people telling each other what to do. For example,

A: "I think you should call the baby sitter to set up the time".

B: "I think you should call; after all, she is your cousin."

A: "Why should I always make the call? You are the one who is going to pick her up."

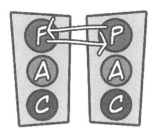

Both people have a clear idea of what the other person should do, and they express it to each other as a "you should" statement. Parent to parent conversations can be productive when each side wants to share his or her private logic. In the example above, person A thinks the other should make the call because he/she is related. The person B responds thinking the other should make the call because he/she will actually be picking up the sitter. Both parties have established reasons why the other person should make the call. How they resolve who will make the call will best be decided if they move to the adult tape and come to an agreement. If they don't go to the adult, then the two parent tapes can command each other with the standoff. Potentially, one person or the other may back down or no action will take place at all.

Adult> Adult Interaction

This form of conversation is typically the most productive. An example I enjoy sharing: a wife asks her husband. "Would you please take the garbage out?"

He responds, 'I'd be happy to once I finish reading the paper."

A request was made, was heard, a time frame for completion was offered and both parties should feel good about the interaction, especially if the husband takes the garbage out when he said he would!

Now what if the wife's question was offered and heard from circles other than the adult. The dialogue might go like this:

"Have you taken the garbage out yet?" (Parent tape 'you should have' implied)

"I'll take it out when I feel like it." (Sounds a bit like a child response to the parent)

Now the couple could have an argument over garbage. Which is not necessarily what they intended to create when the conversation started.

Adult to adult conversations often present helpful information, insights, provide options and offer opportunity for compromise. For example, friend one says,

"Would you like to go to the opera with me on Tuesday or Thursday evening? I have an extra ticket".

"I would love to join you. But I work Tuesday night. How much will the ticket cost?" friend two responds.

"Oh, there is no cost to you. I got these tickets from a person who works at the theater and he said they were really good seats that a client couldn't use. So he offered them to me for free. Let's plan on doing the Thursday performance then."

"Great, I would enjoy that. Why don't you let me drive since you were nice enough to include me?"

"Ok. 7:30 pm work for you? If so, see you then."

Both people were granting each other helpful information as they made their personal offers and finalized their plans.

Summary Concepts

1. We all have Parent-Adult-Child circles/tapes in our lives.

2. Parent tapes often start with the word "You should, You ought...You better, Don't you ever"...These tapes are never erased; however, these tapes can be overruled.

3. Child tapes often sound like "I want...I need...Give me..." or "it's your fault that happened"

4. Adult tapes use expressions like "We could, what do you think, what are our options..."

5. A listener interprets which circle the message is coming from based on not only the words spoken but also past experiences, voice inflection, vocabulary used, tone of voice, non-verbal facial expressions and even body language.

Questions to Consider

1. When you talk with people can you identify a voice you hear yourself speaking from most often?

   a. I think you...(parent tape)

   b. I would like us to consider...(adult)

   c. I want more...(child)

2. Think of a time your conversation ended in an argument. Now diagram which circle you were speaking from to start. Which circle heard the comment? What circle did the responder come from? Which circle heard and interpreted the response?

3. Think of a conversation that was very successful. Now diagram which circle was speaking to start. Which circle heard the comment? Which circle responded?

4. Go back and reframe the conversation in number two. How might the conversation sound if you tried to work exclusively in the adult?

14

CHAPTER 2
THE AWARENESS WHEEL
CLARIFYING ISSUES WITH OTHERS

In 1991 four professors from the University of Minnesota created a curriculum to assist couples in talking and listening together. My wife and I were fortunate at the time to be attending a church that sent us to be trained as instructors in this curriculum. We were impressed with the simplicity of the concepts and yet the insight it brought to human interactions. Although originally designed for couples, a key element of the program was a diagram called the Awareness Wheel. The wheel quickly became a useful tool I found myself using with people in family relationships, work relationships, professional relationships as well as engaged, partnered and married relationships. When two or more people were interacting, the Awareness Wheel offered insights into what was taking place.

The Awareness Wheel looks like this:

At the center of the Awareness wheel is an issue. An issue is defined as anything that needs to be resolved. It doesn't have to be a problem or difficulty. An issue can be as simple as what do I want to eat for lunch? Or an issue can be as significant as do I take the job in Alaska? Issues aren't necessarily good or bad; they are just items that need to be resolved.

Around every issue are five component parts relating to that issue. I like to start at the top of the circle, which is sensory data. Sensory data are the concrete things you can see, hear, taste, touch, and smell.

Next we come to the interpretations. These are based on previous experiences of the sensory data. For example, a person can be sitting in my office in Las Vegas and they might think my office was a very cool 72 degrees. Cool certainly compared to the 103 degrees it might be outside on a summer day. However, if a person could come into my 72 degree office from a walk in freezer, my office would suddenly seem very warm compared to the 32 degree freezer. My office hasn't changed temperature but the interpretation of the sensory data would be influenced by where the person was coming from.

Third, we have our feelings. I always tell folks, that feelings are always 100 % correct. We can never ask someone to stop feeling. We feel what we feel for a reason. And we often feel it based on our interpretations of sensory data. I had a pastor friend years ago who shared a story that explains this relationship. He got on a plane to fly non-stop from LAX Airport in Los Angeles to JFK Airport in New York. He sat down next to a woman who was quietly sniffling. He asked her if she was ok and she nodded yes. About an hour into the flight my pastor friend is feeling really annoyed. The woman is still sniffling and this was in the days before headphones, so he was getting irritated with her persistent noise. As the flight continued the pastor was feeling angry at her insensitivity and he wanted to give her a piece of his mind. Sometime during the second hour of the flight my friend was having violent thoughts such as, I'll give you something to sniffle about lady. His perception of the woman was that she was rude and inconsiderate to her fellow seat mate. As the plane approached the three hour mark, the woman made some small talk and learned that he was a pastor. She trusted him enough to explain her situation. She and her husband had been in LA on vacation. Her husband went golfing with some friends and had a massive heart attack on the golf course. He died in the hospital and his body was in the hold of the plane. She and the body were flying back to New York for the funeral. My pastor friend's feelings changed immediately. He no longer felt anger at her sniffling but sympathy for her grieving. His violent thoughts faded away as he was moved by compassion to empathize with the loneliness and shock that the woman was processing. She was still sniffling (sensory data) but the new interpretation changed his feelings immediately. We can't ask people to stop feeling what they are feeling, but we can ask them what they saw, heard, and perceived that generated that feeling. If we can redefine the interpretation, often the feelings will change.

The fourth element is wants. We all have wants, desires and intentions and our intentions lead us to our actions.

Actions are the fifth and final element around an issue. Our actions become another person's sensory data that they process, interpret, have feelings about, a want to respond that leads to that person's action. We in turn have new sensory data to interpret. And in this way the two people begin to influence each other.

The Awareness Wheel is a great tool to help two people begin to map what is transpiring between them. An engaged couple came in for pre-marital counseling and when they sat down they both turned their backs slightly toward each other and folded their arms. Although nothing was verbally said, the tension they brought into the room was almost tangible.

I shared the observation that they were each in a fairly defiant posture (sensory data) and I felt a tension in the air (interpretation and feeling). Did they have an issue on the way over to the church? They both nodded yes. I asked if they wanted to talk about it. They decided they would.

The unresolved issue: who would pay the bills for their new household? He said he should pay the bills because the Apostle Paul suggested in the New Testament that the man should be the head of the house. The head of the house should pay the bills. Then Jeff turned to the woman he loved and said, "Besides, I will give you all the money you need." The expression on her face went from shock to anger. "I don't need you to give me money. I can manage my own bills just fine." I could see the escalation in emotion for each of them. I asked if they wanted some feedback and they decided they did.

They were both talking about paying bills but they each had a different issue. For Jeff it really was a theological issue. He thought the Bible instructed him to be the head of the house and he should provide for his wife. Julie, on the other hand, was not in a theological discussion at all. For her it was a power struggle. She was a very successful CPA in a large firm and she made a good income and handled all her expenses just fine by herself. As we clarified the situation, they discovered they each had different issues that were sharing data but causing problems for their communication. As we moved around the Awareness Wheel, each person got in touch with his/her issue, and then, we could clarify the data so that their individual issues could be resolved. The couple was able to leave the office holding hands and smiling. A big improvement over the gloomy tension they brought into the room.

The Awareness Wheel allows two people to understand what they are discussing. The first question to always ask is, "What is the issue?"

If both people can agree on what the issue is, then each person can begin to go around the wheel and share: This is what I see, hear you saying, observe going on (sensory data). Next we can share what we think it means (interpretation). That is followed by how my interpretation makes me feel. Then I can express what I want to see happen and finally act. The other person can do the same, and if each person takes the time to listen to the other person, resolution to any issues can be found.

There are times when multiple issues are at play and it may take a while to figure out what is going on. In those situations I find myself grabbing a piece of paper and drawing a circle for each issue that gets mentioned. When the conversation has come to an end, then I try and find out what is the most significant issue holding all the other issues together.

I recall receiving a call from an irate mother. She was angry that her daughter was spending too much time with her boyfriend. (circle 1) The mother thought her daughter was also too busy at work (circle 2). She was also gone too much coaching soccer and playing volleyball (circles 3 and 4). Besides, her daughter wasn't ready to get married (circle 5). Her daughter didn't know how to cook (circle 6). And furthermore the daughter was too young to be serious about life. (circle 7). When the mother concluded her tirade, I asked her which of the 7 issues was the most important to resolve first? When I read the list back to her she sounded confused.

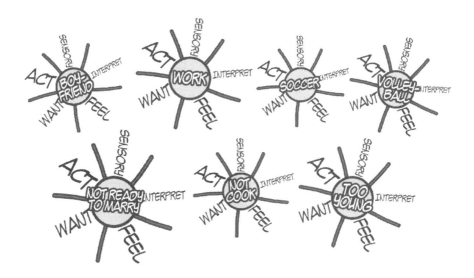

Mom thought her daughter was spending too much time with the boyfriend. But I wondered how much time could the girl be spending with him if she has a job and is coaching soccer and playing volleyball. If the girl didn't know how to cook, who was supposed to teach her? If Mom thought her 19 year old daughter was too young to be married then was there an ideal time to be married in Mom's mind? As I pondered the list it slowly became clear to me. These were all irritating issues to the mom. As I looked at the list I realized that there was one theme they all had in common-- these were all things that Mom wanted to control. The dominant issue was Mom wanted to control every aspect of her 19 year old daughter's life. The driving issue that held all her complaints together was her desire for control.

When I finally addressed the control issue, of course, Mom did not want to admit that was her intention. She was just trying to help her daughter not make any mistakes. When I subtly asked Mom how old she was when she got married, I was not surprised when the Mom shared that she was 19! Ah, the dominant issue was Mom apparently regretted getting married so early and had done everything she could to prevent her daughter from making a "mistake" like hers. Multiple issues take time to unpack. In fact, there is another image that helps me describe the situation to a listener.

I invite the person to imagine a can of Pringle Potato Chips. Every chip is neatly cradled by the one above it and the one below it.

For instance, if you take one chip off the top and place it on the bottom of the pile, and repeat that action as each new chip gets to the top, a single can of Pringle chips can seem infinite. However, if you take each chip off the top and place it on the table we quickly realize that every can of Pringle chips is finite. In a similar way if each chip represents an issue in a person's life, sometimes a person will look at the issue, not resolve it and put it on the bottom of the pile. Then they consider the next issue, don't resolve it and place it on the bottom of the pile. Every group of issues will seem endless and at times overwhelming if they only get placed on the bottom of the pile and never resolved. But if we place each issue on the table, we can see that there are a finite number of issues and the person can choose which issue to work on first, second and so forth.

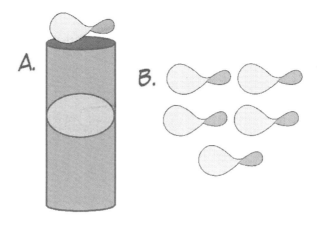

Once a person has determined what all the issues are then it is helpful to determine whose issue is it. There are times that an issue is important to one person but of no importance to the other. Whoever owns the issue should take responsibility for working through the issue. The other person can provide insight, perspective, and feedback.

If, on the other hand, the two people agree that the issue involves each of them there are some further helpful questions to address.

When do we want to work on the issue? Is now a good time or do we need to postpone the discussion, action, until a later date? If it is to be postponed, it is extremely helpful to set a specific time (let's talk about this after we have finished dinner) and not just let it slide with "later".

Once we know when we will address the issue it is helpful to think and talk through how we will know the issue is resolved. In the case of two people deciding on buying a car together, once the car is purchased they will know the issue is resolved. However, if the issue is not as black and white as a purchase then each person will need to agree on what the end might look like.

For example, if the issue is two people want to spend more time together, each person will need to think through his/her definition of "more". If the two people are currently spending 20 minutes a day together would spending 21 minutes a day next week satisfy their perception of more? Technically it is more time. One person might suggest the couple sit in the same room and watch television together and think that was great "more" time together. The other may want to have a date night with dinner and then visit an art gallery and have an in-depth discussion on the merits of the impressionist paintings they viewed. Each person's definition of "more" will need to be clarified for the couple to successfully resolve the issue.

Having determined whose issue it is, when we will discuss it, how we will know it is resolved we are left with one more goal: working toward "win-win" solutions.

Taking the example of the couple in the previous paragraph, each person had a very different perception of what more time together would look like. If only the TV watcher gets his way and the couple spend an evening watching TV in the same room the perception will be he "wins" because his choice for together time was chosen. She, on the other hand, would "lose" because her choice was rejected. Win- lose situations quickly become "lose-lose". If the TV addict gets his way "winning" week after week, it won't be long before the other person will resent the fact that her choice was never given a chance. Although he may be happy thinking all is great since he is enjoying his nights of TV, his partner will eventually want to "get even". He will start to pay in some fashion. Win-lose situations slowly descend into "lose-lose". They will both pay a price in the long run.

The way the couple could resolve their together time issue with a win-win might look like this: One week the two people spend the evening watching TV in the same room and the husband wins that week. The next week the couple might choose to spend an evening having dinner and then attending the gallery of the wife's choosing. Afterward they go for dessert or a drink and discuss the paintings they observed. That particular week the wife wins. If they continue to alternate weeks and each gets a chance to take the lead in what their together night activity consists of, they will have a true "win-win" situation.

Summary Concepts

1. An issue is anything that needs to be resolved.

2. There may be multiple issues at play in a situation. It is always helpful to determine the issue that has the greatest impact on the others and deal with that issue first.

3. Around every issue are five component elements:

    a. Sensory Data: what we can see, hear, taste, touch, smell

    b. Interpretations: based on previous experiences of the sensory data

    c. Feelings: they are always 100 % correct. Do not ask someone to not feel but you can ask what they interpreted and what sensory data they are processing

    d. Wants: our desires and intentions concerning the issue

    e. Actions: our actions become the sensory data that another person picks up with their sensory receptors

4. It is important to determine what is the issue needing resolution

5. It is important to determine who has the most energy about an issue. That person should take the lead in processing the Awareness Wheel.

6. It is helpful to determine when you will talk about an issue. Be as specific as possible.

7. It is important to know how you will know the issue is resolved.

    a. It is helpful to work for win-win outcomes.

    b. It is not helpful to have win-lose outcomes. They are successful in the short term but only for one person. Too many one sided victories can lead to lose-lose outcomes if they are not addressed fairly.

Questions to Consider

1. Make a list of issues that you would like to discuss with a friend, partner, child, parent or spouse. Choose one of the issues and go through the Awareness Wheel filling in each component part about that issue. How might you bring that issue and awareness to the person it involves?

2. Have you ever been the "winner" in a win-lose situation? How did it feel?

3. Have you ever been the "loser" in a win-lose situation? How did it feel?

4. Have you ever successfully found a "win-win" solution to a situation? How did that come about? How did it make you feel?

Chapter 3
THE KARPMAN DRAMA TRIANGLE
HOW TO HELP OTHERS WITHOUT GETTING HURT

There are three common roles people play in stressful situations. The first role is that of the victim. A person who finds him or herself in a predicament that he/she doesn't think he/she could handle by him/herself. Most often, the victim has a person, circumstance or situation that is causing them distress and the cause is the circle called the perpetrator. Having felt the discomfort of the perpetrator, the victim gives off a vibe--it may be in words asking for assistance or it may take the form of non-verbal gestures or expressions that create a sense of helplessness. Sometimes the message is in the form of subliminal messages but regardless, the message is radiated from the victim: help me! The rescuer is a person who picks up the distress signal of the victim and seeks to step in and "solve" the problem, rescue the victim and make everything better.

I draw the triangle this way

It doesn't matter what the problem is really. The victim gives off the SOS and the rescuer picks up the message and looks for ways to come in and assist.

The amazing thing about the Karpman drama triangle, first written about by Stephen Karpman in 1996, in 100 % of the cases once the rescuer comes in and does the rescue, the victim will become a perpetrator and burn the rescuer. One hundred percent of the time! It seems rescuers are slow to learn that if they rush in and do the work for the victim the rescuer will get taken advantage of in the end. The outcome is guaranteed. What does this look like? Let me give you an example.

A young woman wanted to be on her own. So her parents went apartment hunting with her and found a nice one bedroom apartment. They all agreed it would be perfect for her first place on her own. Although she didn't have a full time job, she was hoping to find one and promised she would help pay as much as she could once she knew her trade school schedule. The parents co-signed the lease and paid the first month's rent. The daughter was set up to succeed. Unbeknownst to the family, the daughter was very good at being a victim and she had successfully set up her parents to rescue her. The parents merely thought they were helping their daughter get started. What transpired next took three months to unfold but the order of events shows the triangle at work. It unfolded like this: While the daughter was going to school, she began dating a fellow she met in a group. The dating took priority over the job search and no job was found. The expenses for month two came due and the daughter asked for some "help" until she found that elusive job. The parents reluctantly agreed and unknowingly rescued the unemployed daughter by paying the apartment bills again.

Next, the daughter decided that she needed some elective surgery done (which she had put off for quite a while). You certainly can't start a new job and immediately take time off for recuperation, so the job search was postponed. After the surgery on her foot was complete, she was having a hard time navigating the steps to her second floor apartment since the building she lived in did not have an elevator. The new boyfriend heard her complaints and it appealed to his desire to be a rescuer for his new girlfriend. He gallantly offered his home as a place for the young lady to convalesce. She took him up on the offer. He had the feeling of a white knight taking care of the young damsel in distress. Except, now the apartment was not being lived in at all and yet the rent and utilities had to be covered every month. Who got to pay those bills for the empty apartment? It was certainly not the unemployed daughter healing from her surgery at her boyfriend's house. Instead, it was the parents who had cosigned the lease. The original rescuers who had stepped in to help their daughter get started instead got burned with a year of expenses for an apartment that was unused for nine months.

The daughter was good at being a victim. She had lured her parents to rescue her in the apartment situation. Later she lured the boyfriend to rescue her in the convalescent situation and in the end both rescuers would get burned. This kind of outcome can be expected one hundred percent of the time when the Karpman drama triangle is in play.

For years I watched well intended parents, friends, relatives, spouses, partners and coworkers reach out with the best of intentions to assist someone they cared about. And time after time, I would observe the Karpman drama triangle play out. The well intentioned rescuer would often go way out of their way to assist the victim only to be victimized in the end themselves. I was often perplexed as to how to break the triangle.

Midway through my career it became clear to me that the triangle is unbreakable as long as the rescuer steps in and does the work for the victim. However, if the person in the rescuing opportunity does not step in and do the work, the triangle is broken. I slowly realized there is a fourth position that can be created. It addresses the victim's needs without doing the work for the victim. The helper role was born.

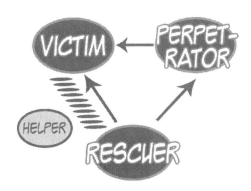

The helper role is one that is characterized by having the same intentions of serving the needs of the victim. However, the helper takes on the unique role of assisting the victim in discerning his/her options. Once the options are clarified, the helper steps back and basically forces the victim to choose which course of action he/she wants to pursue. The helper does not step in and do the work.

Victims are often feeling stuck and they send out the vibe for help because they really are not sure what they can do differently. In fact, in many cases victims portray a sense of helplessness. There is nothing they can do. "Won't you please rescue me?" is the invitation for the rescuer to begin the trip around the triangle to becoming victimized in the end.

As I developed the role of helper with victims, it became clear to me I needed to give victims a sense of hope. There are always options. Of course, the victim will often resist such optimism because they just feel like there is nothing more he/she can do.

What I came to discover over time is that there are always three options to consider. **Option 1:** do nothing. Don't change a thing. Keep doing what you are doing and the results are pretty obvious. The victim is well aware of the situation and that is why they have given off the vibe for help. However, in many cases I would offer suggestions on courses of action the victim might consider and they had a "Yes, but" response to every single one. The victim would counter my suggestions with "Yes, I could do that…but, if I do…"etc. Hearing their resistance to doing anything different I could then summarize, "It appears that option 1 is your choice. You don't want to do anything different, so you know how this will play out just more of the same outcomes" Of course, often the victim doesn't want to hear that their terrible situation is really the result of their own choice. But, as a helper, option 1 best describes the reality for victims who don't want to do anything differently.

Option 2: a person can make some small changes. In the wonderful 1991 comedy film "What About Bob?" Bill Murray plays the multi-phobic victim Bob Wiley and Richard Dreyfus plays the successful psychologist Dr. Leo Marvin. In the movie Dr. Marvin is constantly encouraging Bob to take "baby steps" to get over each of his many phobias. The idea of baby steps is the essence of the option 2 position. In the helper role our task is to help the victim brainstorm some small steps he/she might consider in addressing the issues in life. There may be multiple small steps that could be considered and when I use the diagram I often draw it like this

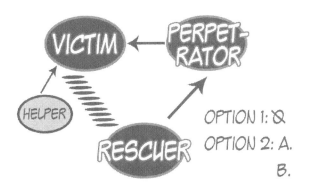

OPTION 1: &

OPTION 2: A.

B.

As the victim and I brainstorm the small steps that might be possible, it is always couched in these are options only if you (the victim) choose to follow through with them. The key for the helper is to only create the list--it must be left up to the victim to choose a course of action from the list.

Option 3: a person can choose to do a lot. These might be drastic measures that carry very large implications for the victim. Again, the role of helper is limited to creating the list of major changes the victim might consider. This list is certainly not binding, but it allows the victim to look at his/her situation and recognize there truly are options to consider. The diagram now looks something like this:

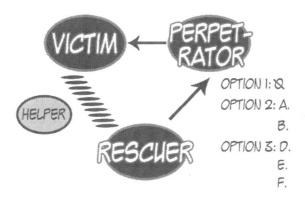

Having arrived at this point in the conversation, the helper can now sit back and let the victim choose the course of action. As long as the helper does not do the work of options 2 or 3, then the person is maintaining the helper role. If, however, the helper steps into the arena and begins to do the work for the victim, then the helper has become a rescuer and the Karpman drama triangle will be reengaged and the rescuer will get burned in the end.

Let's look at an example of the helper role at work. Bryce came to see me because he was very frustrated in his life and marriage. He was in a career he didn't particularly enjoy. His boss at work was constantly on his case about the quality of his work. He would love to try something new and different but he didn't want to leave the security of his current employment. He was tired of his wife making derogatory comments to him as she was constantly "nagging" at him to get a better job and make more money. He would love to make more money but how could he? He already had a mortgage and car payments and kids' needs to be taken care of now. He didn't have any friends he could talk to, and he didn't have any connections for a new job. He needed some help but what could he do?

"Well Bryce", I started, "what would you like to do about all this?" "I don't know," he said, "I feel stuck, could you give me some help?" I drew the Karpman triangle and began to explain the pieces.

"It sounds like you are a victim at work…no options and a boss that is on your case" Bryce agreed. "It sounds like you are a victim at home too…no options and a wife that is on your case". He agreed again. Indeed, Bryce was stuck and as the victim he was sending out strong signals for me to figure out a way to rescue him. I resisted the temptation to fix his predicament. Instead, I took the role of helper and invited him to take a journey with me on each of these issues.

As we looked at Bryce's work situation, I told him he really had at least three options. He got a surprised look on his face and told me he didn't see it.

Option 1…you can do nothing differently Bryce and you can go on being frustrated at your work place.

Option 2…you can choose to do some little things differently. Such as,

   a. Talk to your boss about his complaints and find out what you could do better.

   b. You could ask the boss if there is another position within the company that you could try.

   c. You could talk to a career counselor on your own time and find out if there is an occupation that you might enjoy more.

d. You could look into taking a class at a local industrial institute or community college and learn some new skill sets on your own. You could pursue using the new skills at your current job or you could take those skills to a job you would enjoy more.

Option 3…you could choose to do a lot. Such as:

a. Quit your job today and get away from the boss.

b. Enroll full time in a technical school or college and pursue a career that gets you excited

c. You could look for a new job in a different company and make the jump to a different environment at your earliest convenience.

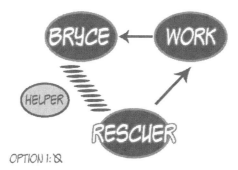

OPTION I: 🔯

OPTION LITTLE: A. TALK TO BOSS

                 B. ANOTHER POSITION AT COMPANY

                 C. TALK TO CAREER COUNSELOR

                 D. TAKE A CLASS

OPTION A LOT: E. QUIT TODAY

                 F. ENROLL IN COLLEGE/TECH SCHOOL

                 G. NEW JOB AT DIFFERENT COMPANY

As the helper I had no vested interest in any of the choices. I merely looked him in the eye and told him he was not stuck at work unless he chose to be stuck. There were 8 options on the table that he could make a decision about. There were certainly pros and cons to each of the options we brainstormed. And when he asked me which one I would recommend? I resisted the temptation to give him a nudge in any direction. Because, if I made a choice of one of the options and he chose to follow it, he would blame me for any negative consequences that might result from that choice. I would have played the role of a helper in creating the list but would have crossed over to being a rescuer by stating a preference. At that point, I would have run the risk of being burned by his disappointment when he followed my "advice," and it didn't work out to his satisfaction.

In a similar fashion we took the issue of his marriage and we created a list for options 2 and 3. He looked at the two lists. One hour before he had come in to my office thinking he was stuck in a job and in a marriage that each had no place to go. After using the Karpman drama triangle with the helper mode included, he still had the same two issues but each issue now had 8 options he could consider. He would stay stuck only if he chose option 1 at work and in his marriage.

I think it is important for the helper to know that it is never a reflection on the helper if the victim chooses option 1. If the victim refuses to try any of the brainstorms, then the victim is choosing to be a victim rather than take ownership of what he/she could do.

My original use of the Karpman Drama Triangle was primarily limited to the roles shared between the victim and the rescuer as discussed earlier in this chapter. Over time, I became aware there was another use of the triangle that was also more prevalent than I would ever have imagined.

I discovered there are people who are professional grade perpetrators and they are constantly looking for people to become their victims. I am not talking about sexual predators; however, that would be an appropriate application of the terms. What I am referring to are men and women who use different approaches to demonstrate their dominance over another person. Let me share two examples of what I mean. One comes from the position of wanting to help.

I had a friend who was in a support group. The purpose of the group was to allow individuals to process the events of their lives in a setting of mutual concern, trust and understanding. The man who happened to run the group was a veteran of many years of doing such group counseling. The incident that was reported to me described a meeting when my friend happened to say that the events in her life were ok that week. There was nothing she needed to process. The response she got from the leader was intriguing to me. He started to question if she was being honest with herself and with the group. He applied verbal pressure on her to dig deep and surely there had to be something that was bothering her. When she replied no, there really wasn't, the leader began to verbally press even harder. My friend felt very uncomfortable that day because she felt the facilitator was trying to lead her into being a victim when she really wasn't feeling it that day. That was the first time I realized that there are people who get accustomed to creating victims. In this case, it was under the guise of helping her dig deep and find something she was subconsciously upset about. The facilitator failed to get my friend into the victim role that day. But the story helped me understand that some folks are best fulfilled in the perpetrator role. And that role can even come from a helping stance.

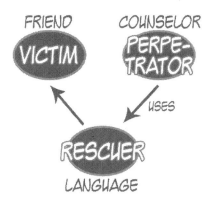

On the other hand, there are professional grade perpetrators who are not coming from the helper role at all. I recall having a phone conversation with a woman who was renting an apartment from a family. The woman called me after she had experienced a very uncomfortable confrontation with the landlord. The landlord had been verbally abusive to her, called her names, and used vulgar language to describe her mother and ancestry. The woman on the phone was very upset and asked me why would a landlord treat her this way?

I described the Karpman Drama Triangle's three roles and asked her which one the landlord sounded like. The woman on the phone was quick to recognize the landlord was a perpetrator. The reality became clear to the woman that the landlord's goal was to make her a victim. The use of a loud shouting voice, name calling, and belittling terms was all in the landlord's arsenal for keeping her in her place. She realized that she had been walking on "egg shells" around the family because she did not want to set off another verbal tirade. The renter who was well educated and confident in the rest of her life was reduced to a fearful victim when she arrived at the apartment. The landlord could be nice at times but always used the threat of verbal abuse to keep the victim in her place. As was true in the earlier use of the triangle, I gave the woman the three options in how she could choose to handle the situation. She could do nothing, a little or a great deal.

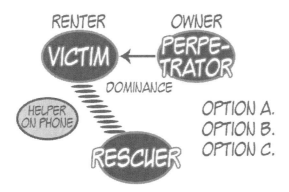

We brainstormed each and then as a helper I stepped back and let her decide how she wanted to handle the situation. The insight for me was the professional grade perpetrator will always have as the goal keeping other people as submissive victims. Helping people deal with such abusive behavior will always come back to giving people hope and options. No one deserves to be a victim. No one.

Summary Concepts

1. The Karpman Drama Triangle applies equally to men and women.

2. In the Karpman Drama Triangle the victim is always feeling discomfort from a perpetrator of some kind. It can be a person, circumstance or situation.

3. In the Karpman Drama Triangle the rescuer is always drawn to make the situation better for the victim.

4. In 100% of the cases if the rescuer comes in and does the work for the victim, the victim will become the perpetrator and cause the rescuer to get burned in some fashion.

5. In the helper role, a person assists the victim in seeing options. Option 1 is to do nothing different; Option 2 is to discern some small steps that can be taken about the issue; Option 3 is to brainstorm some major steps that could be considered on the issue.

6. The helper is advised to not make recommendations on which option to follow

7. The helper is not to be evaluated on which choice the victim makes. The victim must be responsible for his/her own choices.

Questions to Consider

1. Can you think of a time you acted like a victim? Who or what

    was the perpetrator? Who did you seek to have come to your

    rescue?

2. Can you think of a situation where you were the rescuer? Who

    was the victim? How did you get burned in the end?

3. Can you think of a time you were a helper? Who was the

    victim? How many options did you help them consider? How

    did you feel after the victim made his/her choice?

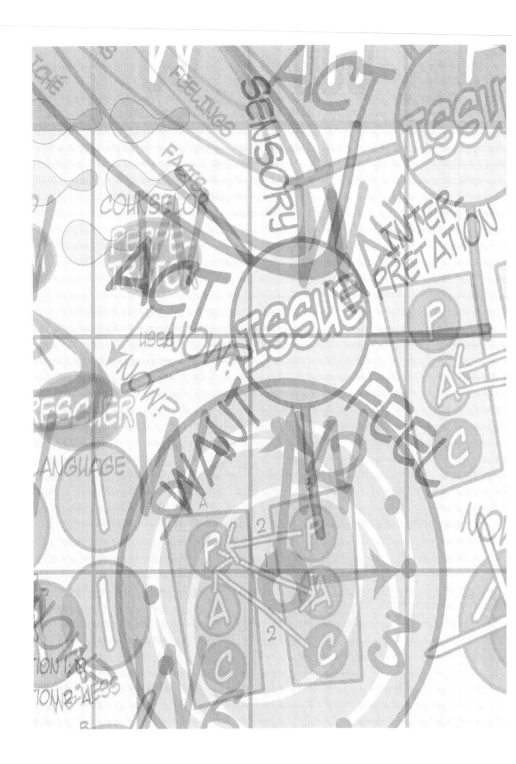

Chapter 4
INTERDEPENDENCE
HOW TO FALL IN LOVE AND STAY IN LOVE

I have had the privilege of performing nearly 700 weddings in my ministerial career. Every couple I have married I have taken some time to have them tell me their story of becoming a couple. Some met each other in elementary school. Others met on the Internet. Some met through friends, relatives, neighbors, coworkers, bosses, employees. Some even met through ex-spouses. I loved hearing each of their stories and I would work hard to make sure a portion of their story made it into my wedding poem homily.

What I discovered over the years of hearing these tales of love was a consistent pattern of how the couple moved from being two independent beings to a couple. The diagram I created starts out looking like this:

As two people get acquainted, there is the excitement of discovery and the anticipation of what lies ahead. When people spend more time together, share their interests and encourage each other to share more time and information, the couple begins to relate the ideas, values, experiences, interests, beliefs or hobbies they have in common. These shared elements become the basis of the overlap of the two individual people. I call these shared experiences "we-ness" goals. They're activities the couple holds in common. The more time and the more elements shared in the we-ness area, the stronger the bond of attraction seems to become. I like to draw we-ness as a shaded area between the two people.

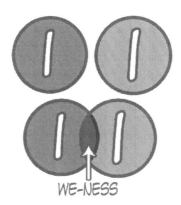

WE-NESS

The longer couples stay together, hopefully, the more elements they may add to their shared we-ness enjoyment. For example, I knew a bride-to-be who was from a family of ballroom dancers. She knew hundreds of steps in the waltz, East and West Coast swing, rumba, cha-cha and numerous other ballroom dances. The groom-to-be knew only how to slow dance and boogie. So as a couple they decided to spend some time together and develop the we-ness of dancing. So they signed up for ballroom dance classes together. He had good rhythm and was motived to learn as many ballroom steps as he could. Together they found a strong bond in both spending the time together and in being able to master a variety of steps. Their we-ness area grew larger.

Sometimes couples share an interest already. Like the bride who loved watching football with her father growing up. When she met a former football player, she not only knew the positions on the team but understood the offensive and defensive strategies. He, being a veteran of the gridiron trenches, loved watching and talking football. As he met the woman of his dreams and learned she loved and understood watching football too, he knew their we-ness would be reinforced by Saturday's and Sunday's spent watching countless games. The we-ness shared made time together fun and encouraging.

Of course there are the couples who seem to have little in common. He may love the excitement of downhill skiing. He might feel fulfillment going at high rates of speed on very steep slopes. She, on the other hand, may hate snow, cold, going fast and dislikes the idea of riding in chair lifts high above a mountain slope. She might be totally comfortable on sandy beaches, sitting in the warm sun and getting tan as she soaks up the sunshine. He, in turn, may hate heat, dislike being wet and only burns when the sun hits his delicate skin. What kind of we-ness can such a couple discover? They may learn to take separate vacations! She can go tan and have a tropical blast. He may need to get some powder skiing in with a group of buddies. Such arrangements are very healthy for keeping each of the "I" aspects intact. But they will need to find some common ground that they enjoy together.

Maybe they both like to entertain other guests. Or they may enjoy cooking or grilling foods together. Or they may both enjoy tasting wine or growing a garden or maybe even doing art projects or working on cars. Every couple needs to find the common ground that enables the we-ness to be sustained and possibly even deepen over time.

The goal is to have shared we-ness time but to never lose that sense of self. There are occasions when one person's interest or personality or position will overwhelm the partner. Such a circumstance can be captured in this way

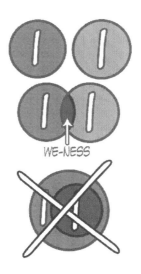

WE-NESS

If one partner becomes completely dominated by the other, that can often lead to a relational disaster--unless the couple happen to be members of a culture where one partner is expected to be dominated by the other partner.

For example, I remember walking down the streets of the Old City section of Jerusalem. I happened to find myself walking next to a woman who was dressed in the modest fashion of a Muslim. I asked her where she was from and she replied Syria. A few moments later, my pace had quickened, and I found myself walking next to a man. I inquired where he was from, and he also replied Syria. I jokingly shared that a few minutes earlier I had just met a woman from Syria. He smiled at me and informed me that was his wife. She was dutifully walking a couple steps behind her husband as their culture dictated.

For that couple, the diagram would make perfectly good sense and would not be cause for alarm at all.

I, however, have grown up in a culture that has put greater emphasis on the equality between the partners and the diagram is the formula for tension if not outright difficulty. The people who maintain the independent "I" of their personality and at the same time have found a good balance of the "we-ness" with his/her partner, those folks will stay in love forever! Each can and will be fulfilled in the relationship.

There are folks who do not manage to maintain the we-ness and slowly the couple experience the shrinkage of their shared life together until all they have left in common may be the same last name and possibly children they are raising together. This process of depleting of the we-ness goals looks like this:

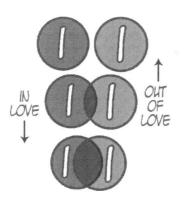

Quite frankly, this is how couples fall out of love. Each person may spend less time with the other, less effort is made to invest in the other person's interests and the result is a growing independence from the other person. Certainly there are relationships where people are ok with living separate lives while residing in the same house or home. There may be economic or emotional reasons for choosing to not terminate the relationship altogether. However, when people are living in just the "I", there are few things that they share in common. They may also become distracted by the arrival of another person, object, habit or addiction that causes the person to move away from the existing partner and begin the investment of time and energy into the we-ness with the new partner.

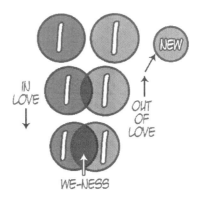

When couples are experiencing difficult times, I often encourage them to list the we-ness activities they have in common. If they don't have many, I suggest they brainstorm some new ones they could acquire and use the list as an outline of we-ness goals they could pursue. If they have an extensive list, I encourage them to quantify how many of those they are currently actively practicing. The majority of the time, couples who are experiencing difficulty have grown lax in the time and energy invested in the we-ness activities. Two people caught up in their individual "I-ness" will often see the we-ness weaken. Without nurture and encouragement the we-ness will surely die.

Summary Concepts

1. All couples start as two people each with an individual "I".

2. It is important that both partners maintain a sense of "I" in the relationship.

3. As people identify activities, ideas, actions, values that they hold in common the sense of "we-ness" is discovered. It must be nurtured and encouraged over the lifetime of the relationship.

4. Usually the goal of a healthy relationship is the balance of "I" and "we-ness".

5. If "we-ness" is not nurtured, it diminishes over time and usually at the expense of the relationship.

6. In times of difficulty it is often helpful to identify and invest in "we-ness" goals.

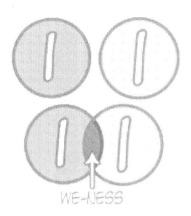

WE-NESS

Questions to Consider

1. Make a list of values and activities you enjoy as an "I".

2. If you are in a relationship make a list of values and activities you enjoy doing with your partner. These are the basis of your "we-ness".

3. If you are not in a relationship but would like to be someday, make a list of "we-ness" activities and values you would like to see in another person.

4. If you have a partner how often do you and your partner invest in the "we-ness" activities?

5. What new "we-ness" activities would you like to try with your partner?

Chapter 5
LANDING LIGHTS
ASSESSING CHANGES IN YOUR LIFE

I am not a pilot. However, I have been flying in airplanes both large and small for years. I have flown in home built ultra-light aircraft, piper cubs, two winged bi-planes, crop dusters, private jets all the way up to 747 jumbo jets. They all have the same issue in common when they have to return to earth. They need to know where to land safely. Most modern large airports have landing lights available to assist the pilot in bringing the aircraft in at the correct altitude.

My initial personal experience with landing lights took place when a friend was taking me on a ride in his single engine Cessna airplane. I was comfortably seated in the co-pilot seat and for the first time getting a chance to see all the maneuvering that goes into landing a plane. We were flying in to an airport that had lights on towers of descending heights as we got closer to the runway. I had driven by those towers hundreds of times having no idea of their significance.

My friend explained that the lights were hundreds of feet apart from each other, and the towers were in descending order with the lowest tower closest to the runway. As we approached and he maneuvered to adjust to the varying wind gusts, he told me the lights on top of each tower needed to form just one solid line. When that line was maintained he was at the correct height to make a safe landing. If, on the other hand, there were two or more lines, then he was either too high or too low and needed to adjust the plane's trajectory accordingly. I watched with fascination as he lined up the lights, eased his craft down and we safely landed at the airport. The experience left a lasting impression on me.

Over the years I started to use this imagery to help me make significant decisions in my life. I found it helpful enough that as I chatted with church members, seminary students, friends, even my own children, I would use the same imagery to help them go about making decisions in their lives as well. How does it work? Here is an example one of my former students shared with me.

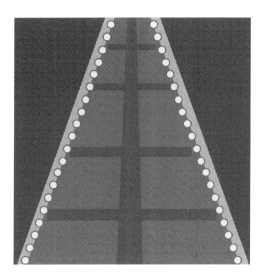

As Derek was getting ready to complete graduate school, he had a couple job offers to consider. I suggested that he create his set of five or six landing lights that would help him decide which job would be the best fit at this time in his life. He came up with the following lights:

- Does the job expect me to use talents and skills that I enjoy using?

- Does the job offer opportunity for advancement?

- Does the job pay enough to live comfortably in that economic market?

- Does the location of the job interest me?

- Is my wife comfortable relocating to that location?

- Is the location a place I am interested in raising a family?

Derek took these six landing lights and used them as he interviewed at each company. When he was done interviewing, he sat down with his partner and they compared lights. Although both companies offered expectations that seemed compatible with his skills and interests, one required a re-location while the other one did not. Both jobs offered about the same compensation but one was in a more expensive market which meant if he chose that place he could not afford the kind of living space he was currently accustomed to enjoying. His wife was not too excited about moving to a different part of the country either. As Derek compared the jobs he realized that the local job offer had all six lights line up fine. That would seem to be a safe landing. The job that required relocation turned out to have a couple lights that did not line up and it would appear to not be a job he should take. Derek took the job that was offered in his home market.

Over the years, I have listened as countless folks created their unique landing lights for all kinds of decisions, which job to take being only one application of the imagery. I have witnessed folks create landing lights to determine when was the best time to get married or have a child. I have listened as folks used this approach to determine if they should expand a business, buy a different house, change churches, find a new place to volunteer, and many other decisions. The key to the process seems to be determining the topics that each light represents.

Summary Concepts

1. Landing lights apply equally to men and to women.

2. Landing lights are well suited for helping a person make a decision. They are particularly helpful when situations require comparing options.

3. There can be as many landing lights as a person may desire. I have often found five or six lights are quite adequate if you choose the best categories for you.

4. The goal of the landing lights is to help clarify the data and assist a person in making an important decision.

Questions to Consider

1. Can you think of a decision you have to make? What landing lights would you create to lead to a safe decision?

2. Can you think of a time when you made a decision that did not turn out well for you? How might the landing lights concept have helped you?

3. Can you think of a time when you made a decision that turned out well for you? Would the landing lights have made the process any easier?

4. Can you think of a situation where the landing light concept would not be helpful to you? Why would it not work?

Chapter 6
THE BLOCK SYSTEM
MAINTAINING BALANCE IN WORK AND LIFE

I've known a few workaholics in my life. Men or women who are committed to working 24 hours a day and 7 days a week if the situation calls for it. As a young pastor I was tempted to be available to my parishioners at all times. In fact, there were a couple early years that I probably was a workaholic. I had no boundaries and at the time, I thought it was what was expected of a pastor. There are lots of occupations that share that kind of unrelenting expectation. Many medical doctors have described to me their residency schedules of working non-stop for two and three sleepless days at a time. They recounted catching short naps in empty rooms and then being in the emergency room diagnosing injuries with major sleep deprivation. Such "war stories" were often shared as if they were badges of honor. In some cases, they were presented as the rite of passage for an intern moving into the role of doctor. I have read stories of football coaches who sleep in their office so they can maximize the time watching video footage of opponents or practices and creating game plans. I have heard male and female entrepreneurs boast about the non-stop vacation-less years they put in to launch their particular company or product line. All these folks shared the willingness to work relentlessly.

In 1992 Doctor Richard Swenson, a practicing physician, wrote a thought provoking book entitled "Margin". In the book he described in vivid detail the exponential changes that have taken place in the lives of Americans. He also described the impact such non-stop changes have had on society as a whole and on individuals. His insights were staggering. I was fortunate to take a graduate school class from Dr. Swenson and that class helped shape a new awareness in my own life. A profound insight came from his simple reminder: "all systems have limits". (Page 74). Those limits may be physical, emotional, or mental for human beings. But those limits will eventually have an impact on our performance limits as well.

It was my desire to begin living a life that was not wall to wall work that started me researching how to live with flexible boundaries. I realized my life had predictable moments of working, eating, and sleeping almost every day. These were forced to share time with my family time, my volunteer time, my personal wellness time, my relational fellowship time, my spiritual growth time and time with my spouse. I wondered how to go about creating a system that allowed for a healthy balance of all these elements against the unpredictable nature of being a pastor to a flock of people whose needs for pastoral care will arise at any moment of any day. It was a daunting task in the beginning. But the block system that emerged brought wonderful balance to an unpredictable life.

The system is based on a simple premise: Every day is divided into three basic parts:

	S	M	T	W	TH	F	SA
A.M.							
AFTER NOON							
P.M.							

The average person who works forty hours a week works a morning block Monday to Friday and an afternoon block Monday to Friday for a total of 10 blocks.

	S	M	T	W	TH	F	SA
A.M.		W	W	W	W	W	
AFTER NOON		W	W	W	W	W	
P.M.							

W = WORK   10 BLOCKS

The remaining eleven blocks of the week can be filled with the many dimensions and interests a person chooses.

There are many occupations, like mine, that do not have an orderly same ten blocks every week. One summer during college I worked at a Gulf Oil gas station on the Pennsylvania Turnpike. The job was very interesting because I never worked the same schedule two weeks in a row. Because the station was open 24 hours every day of the year, we employees were given some crazy schedules. Using the block system, here was one of the weeks I worked:

	S	M	T	W	TH	F	SA
A.M.	W		W			W	
AFTER NOON		W	W	W		W	W
P.M.		W					W

10 BLOCKS = 40 HOURS

As you can see, I only worked ten blocks (10 blocks x 4 hour blocks = 40 hours) but those hours were spread out all over the 21 possible blocks. This is where the block system got its start for me. I realized that I could structure my work life in such a way that I always worked my appropriate number of blocks but they could reflect the unpredictable nature of a pastor's life.

As I moved along in my career I realized that I was more accurately working a six day work week. That meant that twelve blocks would be the appropriate number to reflect the 48 hour work week that seemed to be standard. At the beginning of each week I would take a look at the calendar and determine which blocks I needed to fill with the given appointments, classes or meetings that week. Next, I would assess which blocks would be available for the walk in appointments, unexpected meetings and preparation for sermons etc. Finally, I would determine which blocks would work for family, spouse, friends, and personal work outs. A week might look like this:

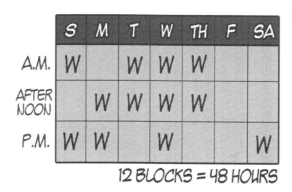

	S	M	T	W	TH	F	SA
A.M.	W		W	W	W		
AFTER NOON		W	W	W	W		
P.M.	W	W		W			W

12 BLOCKS = 48 HOURS

At other times, when my family had major events going on in their lives I would look at the week and start by putting in the significant dance recitals, swim meets, skating competitions or basketball games that needed my attendance. Then I would fill in when work would best be done. Those blocks looked like this:

	S	M	T	W	TH	F	SA
A.M.	W		W	W	W		F
AFTER NOON		W	W	W	W		F
P.M.	W	W	F	F	F	F	W

W = WORK   F = FAMILY

In either calendar I was always fulfilling my duties as a full-time employee. However, I was managing my work to fit my overall obligations. The system works wonderfully.

I remember doing a consultation with a congregation that was experiencing a fair amount of tension between the office staff and the program employees. The office staff worked the typical ten blocks Monday to Friday 8am to 5 pm work week. The program staff, however, would take off for lunch for two hours and office staff resented the fact the other employees could be gone for so long at lunch. When we had a staff meeting I addressed the tension, I introduced the block system to the entire staff. I invited the staff members to fill in which blocks they were working. The office staff dutifully filled in their blocks and they looked like this:

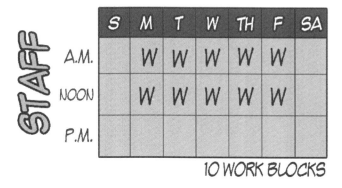

When the program staff filled in their blocks the youth director's schedule looked like this:

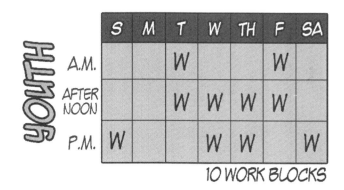

When the music director filled in her blocks they looked something like this:

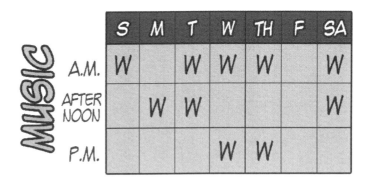

What the office staff finally observed, their ten blocks were defined and regular. They worked the same ten blocks every Monday to Friday. But the program staff had work blocks all over the week. When the youth director was busy on Wednesday night with confirmation classes from 5 pm to 9 pm, the office staff members were quietly at home. When the music director was busy leading the choir on Sunday morning the office staff members were not on the job. The fact that the program staff went out for a long lunch did not mean they were not working 10 blocks that week. Rather, it meant the program staff members were working a different ten blocks. The tension between office and program staff disappeared. Everyone was working hard, just at different times.

I have long encouraged employees with flexible scheduling issues to keep track of the blocks required each week and then mix and match one block for another. For example, once a month I have a church council meeting that convenes at 5:30 pm on a Wednesday evening. That block is normally reserved for family time. However, when the first Wednesday of the month rolls around and I know the council will be meeting, I purposely choose a block I normally work and then don't work it. The simple illustration would be on council meeting Wednesday I don't start my work day at the office in the morning block. Instead, I might stay home and spend time with the family and start my work day that week at noon knowing I will be engaged in work well into the evening. These simple changes can also come on weeks when I might have a hospital emergency on my day off. No question I need to be there and fulfill my duties. However, later in the week I can take a normal work block off and balance my life a little better.

I have taught this simple system to interns, business leaders, fellow pastors, medical personnel and anyone else who would listen. It has provided the mechanism to balance work and the rest of life in a simple yet meaningful way.

Summary Concepts

1. The block system works equally well for men and women.

2. In the basic system every day has three blocks and every week has 21 blocks.

3. Weeks can be exactly the same or radically different. In either case the number of blocks spent in work, family time, recreation, personal growth, fellowship time, volunteering, eating and sleeping can all be adjusted based on individual preference, skill set or obligations.

4. In some cases, I have observed people divide work days into six 2 hour blocks. The 40 hour job now requires 20 blocks. This adaptation allows for more precise dividing of time spent in each activity. Be creative and use whatever system works for you.

Questions to Consider

1. Take a look at your typical week of activities. How much time is spent in work? In recreation? In personal commuting? In relationships? In hobbies? In watching television? In computer/texting/tweeting? Other activities?

2. As you look at the time spent in number 1, what would you like to change and do less?

3. As you look at number 1, which item would you like to increase?

4. What prevents you from making changes in your schedule?

Chapter 7
LEVELS OF COMMUNICATION
CHOOSING THE STYLE THAT WILL SERVE YOU
BEST

In 1969 John Powell wrote a wonderful paperback book entitled:"Why Am I Afraid to Tell You Who I AM?" It was a very helpful guide as I began my ministry career. One of the key concepts I learned from the priest who turned into a best-selling author was the importance of knowing what style of communication to use in any given moment in time.

Over the years, I have used these levels of communication extensively as I sought to communicate with audiences big and small. I have often described these levels as invisible hula hoops that radiate away from our body.

There are five of these concentric circles radiating around us. Let's address them in the order that we would encounter them with a person.

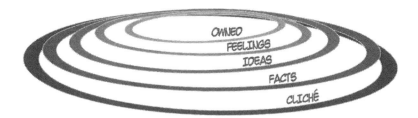

First Level

The first level is the cliché level of communication. "Hi, how are you?" Fine, what are you up to?" It is the safest, least vulnerable level we can offer another person. We are acknowledging the presence of another human being without any risk of self-disclosure.

Second Level

The second level of communication is the factual level. This level of communication invites the sharing of information. Each person is able to determine how much information he/she shares at this level. "Where have you been?"

"I have been up at the cabin for the past few days. We had beautiful weather." Interest is shown by the inquiry and the responder can choose what level of information to disclose.

Third Level

The third level of communication is called the ideas level. It is at this point that the people involved begin to share their personal thoughts.

"What did you think of the election results?"

"I really don't like the winning candidates stand on taxation."

The questioner invited an opinion and the responder shared exactly what was on his/her mind. Ideas level of communication can be supportive of people or causes that a person agrees with or negative toward issues or people they disapprove. Ideas are the first level of communication where there may be disagreement. People with contrasting opinions can rant and rave here sharing their opinions and let their disagreements be known to each other or the world listening to them.

Fourth Level

The fourth level of communication is described as the feeling level. It is at this level that a person begins to share his/her feelings.

"What did you think of the election results?"

"I was devastated."

At this level, a person moves past the cliché's, past the facts, past the ideas and begins to share the heart and soul of feelings. This is a very vulnerable level since we can never be sure how people will respond to our honest feelings.

"What did you think of the election results?"

"I was devastated."

"Really? I didn't think it was such a big deal. Why are you so emotional about it?"

To have shared on a feeling level and have our feelings belittled would not be pleasant.

"What did you think of the election results?"

"I was devastated".

"Really? Why was that so hard for you?"

"My preferred candidate is a very good friend and I am so sad that she lost the election. I tried to do everything I could to get her elected."

At the feeling level, we always take a risk in sharing our feelings. Sometimes they are met with empathy or even sympathy. At other times, our feeling level may be met with disdain or criticism. We can never be sure which we will get especially if we do not know the person very well.

Fifth Level

The fifth and final level of communication John Powell called the "owned" level of communication. This is us: our sincere values and most treasured ideals. We tend to not share these with too many other people. This is the core of our being and we protect this level a great deal. In fact, we will not share this level unless there is a great deal of trust with a person.

The levels of communication serve as invisible protective barriers and we filter other people through these levels. We can share cliché's with anyone on the street. We will share our facts with a smaller number of people. Still fewer will ever get to hear our ideas. Far fewer will ever experience our emotions, and finally precious few will ever know the majority of our owned perceptions. On one hand the invisible hula hoops keep people at a safe distance until we get to know them better.

The crucial ingredient that allows us to move a person from one level to the next deeper level is trust. Trust, I would define as being comfortable that the person will not use or abuse the information. As we are confident that the person invited to go deeper will handle the disclosure in confidence and respect, we often take the risk and move to the next level.

If, however, a person misuses the information or emotions shared, that person is often expelled from that level of communication.

How can this information be useful in life situations? I have made it a practice to take my time whenever I meet someone. I am seldom in a hurry to get to the next level of interchange. If, over a period of time, I get a sense that I can trust them, then I invite them to the next level through my own disclosure.

Over the years, I have observed that most people function by opening themselves to another person slowly. There are always the exceptions, for example, a person may ask a cliché question "How are you today?" and the recipient begins to offer a ten minute monologue on all their pains…sharing their facts ("I went to the doctor today and had a colonoscopy".) Then they begin to share their ideas ("I just think the medical profession is a bunch of crooks. All those doctors want to do is collect their checks and give as little time to the patient as possible.") Then share their feelings ("I hate how impersonal the nurses were when I got my results. I was really scared by what they told me"). Wow. All I asked was a cliché question and then I got a response on all levels. If we know the person well we might expect such honesty. If we don't know the person well we are often taken back by such rapid self-disclosure.

On the other hand, we may encounter a person for the first time who immediately wants to get into our owned space. "Hi pastor. Say, I know we are at a wedding, but I have always wanted to ask a preacher why does God allow so much evil in the world?" The person made no effort at self-disclosure. In addition, he ignores the joyous setting of a wedding and plunges in to the complicated theological inquiry expecting me to satisfy his inquiry with my facts, ideas, possible feelings and owned faith. I usually give them a cliché response like "I'd be happy to chat about that at another time. Why don't you give me a call next week and we can set up a time to discuss your question." If they are really serious about the inquiry they will call. If they don't call, I figure they didn't really want my answer anyway.

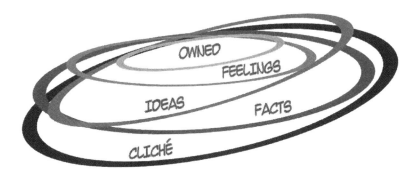

Certainly a person can begin speaking from whatever level he/she chooses. I have walked into hospital rooms, and the family members immediately begin speaking from the feeling level if they have a loved one in critical condition. Or walking into a courtroom, the judge may immediately move to the factual level in trying to determine what happened at the scene of the infraction. A professor may begin a lecture by sharing his/her ideas about the political science situation in the state senate. A scientist may start his/her conversation on the importance of an experiment by sharing his/her owned perceptions of what the research means to science. There is no correct level to start or stop. It will always be a decision we as individuals need to make. As the speaker I must decide which level I want to start in and determine if there is a desired level I would like the conversation to attain. When I begin my conversation at the chosen level my listener must determine what level I am coming from and then is there a level he/she would like to respond. It is an interesting process that is part of every human conversation.

Once we have started the conversation, sometimes the levels can go in a fairly straight line.

"Hi, how are you?" (cliché)

"Fine, what's up?" (cliché)

80

"Did you hear I had an accident with Penny last night?" (Fact)

"No, I did not hear that. Was it serious?" (Fact)

"Yeah, I think it was the fault of my right tire. It must've blown." (Idea)

"No kidding? What kind of tire was it? How fast were you going?" (Fact)

"I don't know the brand. All I know I was really scared when I heard the pop and the car began to swerve." (Feeling)

"I am so sorry to hear that happened. Were you hurt at all?" (Feeling)

"No, luckily. However, I feel so bad that I put Penny through such a frightening experience. She is one of my best friends and I wouldn't want to hurt her." (owned)

Other conversations may go all over the place depending on how each person decides to respond.

"Hey, how are you?" (cliché)

"I'm not in the mood to talk, ok? Just leave me alone." (Feeling)

"Sorry, you don't have to be so snippy about it." (Idea)

"I'll be as snippy as I want. I had a horrible day and I don't want to talk to anyone." (Fact)

"Ok, no skin off my nose." (cliché)

Some conversations will find one person staying in the same level while the other person works hard to move them on.

"Hey, what's up?" (cliché)

"I'm so glad you asked. I really wanted to talk to you about a situation." (idea)

"Who'd you want to talk about? Sounds like fun." (Cliché)

"No, I'm serious, this isn't meant to be gossip-- I have some real concerns." (feeling)

"No, I get it. Let's hear the skinny, who is it?" (Cliché)

"Come on man, I'm not joking around here." (idea)

"Ok, ok. Get it out, I can't wait all night." (cliché)

I have found this particular tool helpful in mapping conversations. For example:

In an interview:

- What level did the interviewer use to start?

- What level should I use to respond to each question?

- What level would best summarize where we should end up?

In a counseling setting:

- I often try and work my way one level at a time beginning with the cliché level.

- I think my goal is to get to the feeling level, but the person's response determines how fast I can proceed.

- I cannot control what level of comfort or trust the client feels with me. Therefore, I don't evaluate myself on the basis of what level of communication we attain.

In a speaking setting:

- I often begin with facts that can grab people's attention.

- I frequently will go to ideas that I want to get across.

- I appreciate when the listeners pick up on the emotion of the moment and spend some time with their feelings.

- I cannot predict if or how a crowd of individuals will respond and at what levels.

- I need to always prepare a talk or sermon in such a way that a variety of levels of communication are utilized. That insures as many people as possible can access the information they heard.

Summary Concepts

1. There are five levels of communication: Cliché, facts, ideas, feelings, owned.

2. We each choose a level to begin every conversation.

3. Our listeners must determine our level and then choose the level in which they want to respond.

4. Speakers can choose what level they would like the conversation to attain.

5. Listeners can choose which level they want to attain.

6. Speakers and listeners can work together or counter one another. It is always a choice.

Questions to Consider

1. Can you think of a dialogue in recent days that started in cliché and ended in the owned level?

2. Is there a level you feel most comfortable starting conversations in?

3. Is there a level you feel the most discomfort sharing with another person?

4. Is there a level of communication that you enjoy sharing with other people?

5. Is there a level of communication that you absolutely avoid?

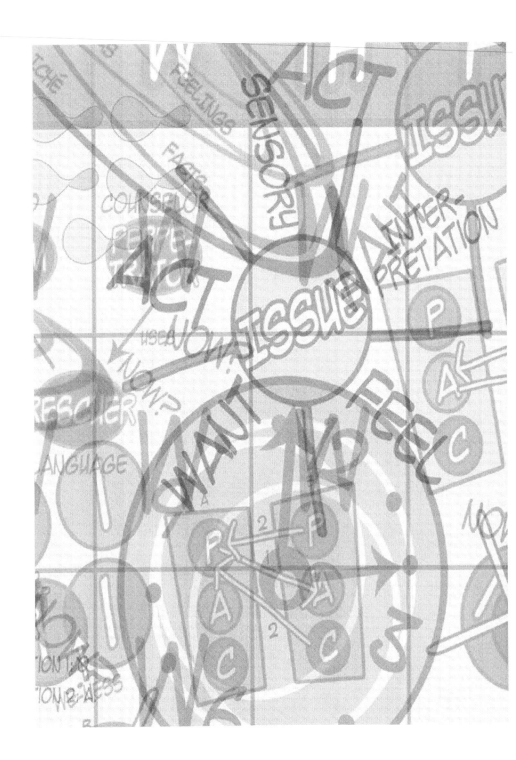

Chapter 8
HEALTHY GRIEF
DISCOVERING THE GOOD THAT CAN COME
FROM A DIFFICULT SITUATION

Americans do not tend to deal with death very well. My experience is that most people in our culture have the attitude that they must be strong after a loved one dies. And in the effort to look strong many folks fail to do the work of grief.

When I meet with a family after the death of a loved one I always tell them we are going to take a few minutes to talk about how to grieve the loss in a healthy fashion. I draw the following diagram.

The death of a loved one is a hand grenade that blows a hole in our emotional life. I have listened as people apologize for crying. Or they chastise themselves for showing any emotions. I tell folks if they try and act strong...they are marching around the hole and failing to do the work of grief. This means that in a month, six months or a year they are no further along in the grieving process than the day the person died.

If, however, a person does the work of grief, then each day is a step away from the hole. And in the course of time, the pain will diminish. What is the work of grief? Being honest with what we are feeling when we feel it. By honestly owning our emotions when they show up, we actually do facilitate our own healing.

I was 24 years old when my father died suddenly of a heart attack, nine days into his early retirement. At 62, he was supposed to live a bunch of years, and he and my Mother were going to do travel and things they had put off for so many reasons. When he died, I knew nothing about the grieving process. This diagram had not been created in my mind. I tried my best to be the strong only child for Mother, composed seminary graduate for my extended family, for my neighbors and friends. It was horrible trying to hold back the tears, the anger, and emotions as they percolated to the front of my consciousness only to have my mind slam them back into the recesses of denial. I was living the diagram above.

I recall driving along the road, and over time, I learned to carry a towel in the car with me. I could never predict when it might happen, but a sight, a sound, a smell, a song on the radio would suddenly trigger an emotional response in me. There were numerous times I chose to pull to the side of the road and bury my face in the towel and cry my tears out. It might last a minute or two, and then I would feel better put the towel down and drive on. At first, I thought I was going crazy. Why is this happening? I would later discover this is how we get better. We need to own the feelings we are feeling when we feel them. As we do, we eventually heal.

Every day that we own the feelings is a day taking a healthy step away from the hole. Eventually the hole will seem smaller. It never changes size. But with time and distance, it will appear to be smaller. This is a very healthy process. The process is no different for men than it is for women. Although our culture likes to portray men in the stoic "John Wayne" tough guy image, in reality men need to do the work of grief as much as women need to do it.

I also discovered that such episodes of emotion came like waves. I could not predict when or how strong they might be, but they would ebb and flow like waves on the ocean. That was when I discovered the next part of the grieving diagram.

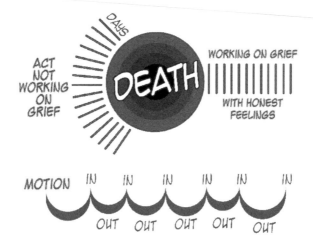

The strength of the wave was unpredictable. There were times it was so strong that it would force me off the road (as I mentioned earlier). There were other times it was merely a ripple of emotion that disappeared as quickly as it had come. Sometimes the emotion was anger --why did my dad die? Why didn't he take better care of himself? At other times, the emotion was sadness--he would never hear me preach a sermon, see me get married or hold any of his four future grandchildren. He would never see the houses I would live in or the churches I would serve. How could he do this to me? Yes, there was a wide range of emotions that I eventually identified from his untimely death. However, as I spent time honestly owning the emotions, they slowly faded away.

It is important to keep in mind that every person grieves in his/her own way. Some individuals are very emotive and tears and wailing are comfortable ways to release the pain. Others may do so quietly. Some shed tears, some do not. There is not a uniform code of grieving conduct that everyone must agree on. However, everyone needs to do grieving and own the feelings they are experiencing. How those feelings are expressed to others is really going to be a matter of personality and personal preference.

I would eventually discern that the healing process had trigger points that created predictable emotional responses in the future:

The first Christmas, first Easter or first family reunion after a death can also trigger an emotional response. Again, over time, if each emotional wave is allowed to break over the heart, then the next one is a little easier to bear.

I have also discovered that if children are involved in the grieving process, they will often revisit the death every time they go through a developmental change. If a loved one died while a student was in elementary school, you can expect they might reprocess the death when they get to junior high. Probably reprocess it again as senior high students and quite possibly again as they enter adulthood. In other words, we should not be surprised that a death that took place years ago may need to be reprocessed as a son or daughter matures emotionally, is able to identify and own more emotions and does the work of grief.

We have been using the grief model as if it only applies to the death of a loved one. However, that is certainly not true. The loss can also be the death of a relationship, (through divorce, for example) or the death of a dream, the loss of a job, the loss of one's health through an accident or illness. The principle remains the same: Whatever form the loss takes, that hand grenade blows a hole in our emotional lives, and we suddenly have the need, and opportunity, to grieve.

Summary Concepts

1. Grief is an important emotional journey that is just as relevant for males as females.

2. Everyone grieves at his/her own pace. We should resist trying to force people to grieve in a certain time frame or expecting others to grieve exactly the way we do.

3. Grieving comes and goes in unpredictable waves. We should allow the wave to roll at its own pace and then own the feelings that come our way.

4. We don't need to be strong for anyone else. Just honest with owning our feelings.

5. Grief may need to be revisited as children mature.

Questions to Consider

1. Using the diagram, how would you describe how you handled the most recent death of a loved one?

2. As you consider doing the work of grief, which emotion(s) are the easiest for you to consider sharing with others?

3. As you consider doing the work of grief, which emotion(s) are the most challenging for you to consider sharing with others?

4. As you ponder the loss of something important to you, which diagram seems to offer the most hope for how to cope with the loss?

Try drawing the diagram while verbally sharing an explanation of each portion so that you could share it with a friend or loved one.

Chapter 9
PRACTICE PUTTING THE PARENT, ADULT, CHILD VISUALS TO WORK

Case One: Parent Adult Child

Let's try a couple conversations and you can practice charting where the conversation is coming from and going to between persons A and B. Draw two rectangles with the P A C circles in each. Then keep track of the conversation using numbered arrows to go between circles.

I will offer some guidance after each dialogue.

Conversation 1

A1: Hey B, why is that material not put away yet?

B1: I thought you were going to do it.

A2: No, you need to put it away.

B2: I can't do it now; my truck is full. I could do it after lunch if you can wait that long.

A3: As long as you get it done today, that will be fine.

How did you do? Let me offer my suggestions on how the dialogue could be charted:

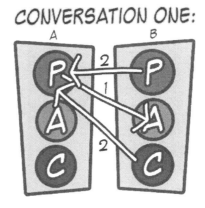

A1: Clearly starts out from the Parent circle. "You should have" is implied in the question.

B1: The response could be from either the child tape "why should I do it?" Or it could be from the Parent tape "I thought you were going to do it".

CONVERSATION ONE:

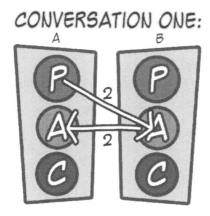

A2: A stays in the Parent tape and lets the directive be clear, B, you are supposed to do it.

> B2: B shifts to the Adult circle. He offers an explanation on why he can't do it now and then offers a time frame for the successful completion of the task.

CONVERSATION ONE:

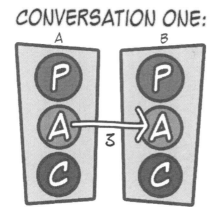

A3: Sounds like he begins in the parent but moves to the Adult circle in accepting the compromise offered.

Conversation 2

A1: B, you should have been at the concert last night.

    B1: I had other plans already in place.

A2: Well, you should have changed them and made the concert your priority. It was very good.

    B2: Who are you to tell me what to do?

A3: Well, you should have come to the concert. People were expecting you.

    B3: That's funny because no one mentioned the concert to me. Who are the people who asked about me?

Let's see how this one might be charted:

A1: A is clearly coming from the Parent circle. "You should have come" is obvious.

    B1: B responds in the Adult by offering a simple explanation for the previous plans

CONVERSATION TWO:

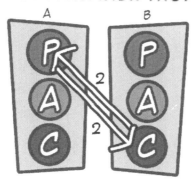

A2: A stays in the Parent circle and is even more directive as to what B should have done

> B2: B clearly responds in the Child. A form of "don't you tell me what to do!"

CONVERSATION TWO:

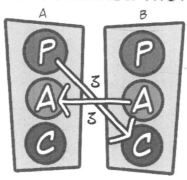

A3: A remains steadfast in the Parent circle

> B3: B moves to the Adult by asking for clarity. B stays in the Adult by stating the fact that no one had mentioned the concert to B before-hand. B concludes by asking A to name the people who supposedly were expecting B's attendance. An Adult inquiry of a possible guilt trip A wanted B to feel.

Conversation 3

A1: Did you happen to notice where I put my tablet?

B1: No. Did you lose it again? You are so absent minded.

A2: I had it last in the study, but I looked around in all my usual places and just didn't see it.

B2: Well, you probably forgot it because you are doing too many things at the same time. You need to slow down.

A3: Thanks for nothing! Could you help me look for it instead of just criticizing me?

B3: You don't have to be so touchy. Did you check in your car?

Let's examine how to chart this last conversation

A1: A is in the Adult and asks an honest question.

B1: B responds in the Parent circle using a bit of sarcasm. Then A adds a judgmental "you" statement at the end.

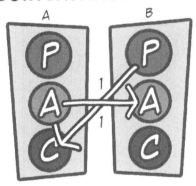

CONVERSATION THREE:

A2: Staying in the Adult, A offers some more factual data.

B2: B responds in the Parent circle first, ignoring the issue of the missing tablet. B goes on to criticize A on the use of time--a Parent circle implied "you should be doing things differently".

CONVERSATION THREE:

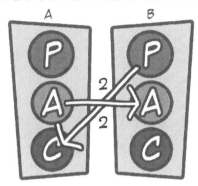

A3: A starts in the Child circle with a sarcastic response. Then A moves back to the Adult and asks for assistance on the missing tablet. A also requests B refrain from commenting on A's lifestyle or use of time.

B3: B starts in the Parent circle..."you shouldn't be so touchy". Then B moves to the Adult circle in brainstorming another place to look for the tablet.

CONVERSATION THREE:

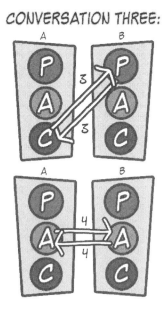

As you look at future conversations, it is helpful to keep in mind that the movement between circles can take place very quickly in the same sentence or paragraph.

Use this space to practice tracking recent conversations.

Conversation 1

Conversation 2

_____

_____

Conversation 3

Conversation 4

_____

_____

Chapter 10
CASE STUDIES
PRACTICE USING THE AWARENESS WHEEL

I invite you to go back to chapter two and remind yourself of the component parts of the awareness wheel. I suggest you duplicate the wheel on a piece of paper. Now I encourage you to read through the following counseling situation that I described and fill in the data on the wheel as it becomes apparent in the case study. I will offer some of my observations periodically during this exercise. Is your awareness wheel ready? Start taking your notes.

Remember the story of the young couple who came into my office for their pre-marital counseling session? When they sat down, I observed some unusual behavior. Each person chose to sit with his/her back toward the other, and they both simultaneously folded their arms. The expression on their faces seemed to communicate some displeasure. There really seemed to be an air of tension in the room. I couldn't be sure if they were unhappy to have to visit with me, or if they had experienced an issue on the way to my office. Having made these observations in my mind, I decided to start the conversation.

I greeted them and then let them know I had observed some unusual behavior. I listed for them what I had observed: the body language of being ever so slightly back to back and each with his/her arms folded. I also told them that I sensed a tension in the room, and I shared my desire to know if they were upset at having to speak with me, or if there was an issue they had experienced on the way to the church. They each looked at me. Jeff spoke first and let me know they had experienced an issue on the way to the appointment. I asked if they were interested in talking about the issue with me. After a few moments of thoughtful silence, they each nodded yes: they would like to address the issue.

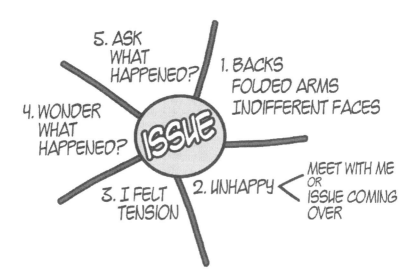

Observations thus far:

We have no idea what the issue is at this point. We do know that something has caused each person to be in a defiant posture. What sensory data did you observe? I hope you noticed they sat with their backs toward each other, they folded their arms and they were acting very indifferent toward one another. This is very unusual behavior for a couple about to get married. Most couples come into this appointment holding hands, smiling, nervously touching each other for support as they get ready to tie the marital knot. My interpretation of the data was that either they were unhappy about having to meet with me or they had an issue that was unresolved as they came into the session. My feeling was of a tension in the room. My want was to discern what had caused this choice of actions. My action was to ask the question. Hopefully you see how the information fit the wheel to this point. Now let's see how the information proceeds as we discover the issue or issues.

Jeff spoke first again. He shared that in the car ride over the two of them had started to discuss who was going to pay the bills once they were in one household. Jeff had told his fiancé that he should pay the bills because he was the head of the house. He suggested that he should be head of the house based on Paul's words in the Bible's New Testament. He was sincere in wanting to fulfill the Biblical mandate of being the head of the house. Then he turned to his bride to be and said with great passion, "and I will give you all the money you need." The expression on her face at that moment was utter contempt. She spoke for the first time and with incredible controlled force responded 'I don't need you to give me money. I manage my money just fine and I can take care of my own bills. I have been successfully taking care of myself for years and I don't need your help!" The tone was firm and defiant.

Additional Observation:

Did you catch that Jeff brought up several different issues? However, he thought they were just one. The first issue was who was going to pay the bills in the new household. The second issue was theological; he interpreted the Apostle Paul was telling him to be the head of the house. The third issue was Jeff's assumption that as head of the house and bill payer, he should be in charge of all the money.

For him, that meant he would basically give Lisa an allowance.

For Lisa, the issue was power. She did not want to feel powerless. She had her own money, and she did not need Jeff giving her funds, no matter how gallant he thought he was being. Their conversation started out talking about paying bills, but five different issues were at play all using the same data.

Hearing all the issues at play, I took out a piece of paper and drew a circle for each of the issues.

His Circle=pay bills   **His Circle**=theological   **Her Circle**=power

His Circle=charge of money   **His Circle**=allowance Lisa

I asked if they wanted to work through the issues toward a win-win solution. They both eagerly said yes. So we moved ahead.

Looking at the five issues it became clear to us that paying the bills was not really the most important issue. Lisa could care less if she sent the mortgage check for the house each month. She did care that she had some control over the money that she earned and spent. We decided that we would look for the best way for this couple to empower each of them to feel like an equal partner in the financial relationship.

We came upon this resolution: They would create a household account complete with the big industrial size checks. Both of their names would be on the checks, and although either of them could write checks from the account, Jeff would take primary responsibility for paying the household bills. Both parties would put their entire employment checks in the household account every month. They were beginning to function as a team for the first time in their shared financial experience. Lisa in particular needed to feel empowered financially. So they agreed to set up individual checking accounts. One account for just Lisa and the other account for just Jeff. Each person would draw an identical amount of money each month out of the household account for just their personal use. She could spend the funds any way she wanted, and he could do the same. The win-win was complete. All of their issues were resolved in a satisfactory fashion. Each person was satisfied that his/her issues had been addressed.

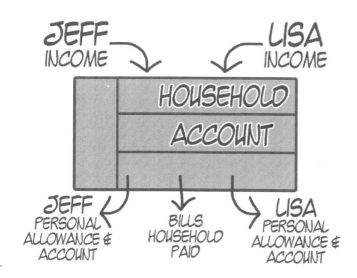

Win-win solutions are always the best. However, there are times people don't choose to take the time to determine the issues and work for each person's satisfaction. What gets created then are what I call Win-Lose situations. These are characterized as one person gets what he/she wants and the other person does not. One wins, the other loses. Over time if the same person always loses, there can be long term consequences, which I call lose-lose.

For example, I knew a couple who had been married for over 14 years. He was a successful business man and built a very lucrative company. During the years of building the company, he abdicated a great deal of the home responsibilities to his wife. "I don't care-- you decide" was a common phrase he used when she asked him for his opinion on everything from household products, paint colors for a room or when to celebrate birthdays and anniversaries. The wife was certainly willing to make the choices he didn't seem to care about. She made the choices she liked and in so doing was a consistent winner. He "lost" by not participating in the decisions. Over time what seemed like a path of little resistance began to create issues. Finally one day the husband came in and announced he wanted a divorce. His wife was stunned. Why on earth would you want that she inquired? "I am tired of you always getting your own way" was his reply. Although he chose to not have an opinion all those years, he eventually held it against her that she went ahead and made decisions. Her winning and his losing, even if by choice, created a lose- lose situation. Their divorce was a loss for each of them in the end.

Over the years I have come to a simple suggestion that I pass on to folks when they have to resolve an issue. The person with the most energy about the issue should consider doing the research, but both partners should strive to be active in making the decision.

A case in point for me was during our engagement, my fiancé inquired what kind of china dishes I wanted. I responded I didn't want china! Fancy dishes were not on my list of things to own. However, that presented a bit of an issue as my family members and even some friends got on my case about it. So I thought about saying, "I don't care you decide," but fortunately for us, I didn't. Instead, I invited my fiancé to go look at china, and when she had five finalists, I would agree to go look at the choices. I have no idea how many stores or patterns she explored, but I do know the fateful Saturday came when I had to go look at the finalists. The first pattern looked ok, but the cup handles were small and I couldn't get a finger in the space. I hated that! Next pattern was too flowery for my taste, so, I didn't want that one either. The third set had good cup handles, elegant but simple design and I really liked them. The fourth and fifth considerations did not surpass number three. We agreed on pattern three. We had our first major win-win experience. She had five she liked, and it turns out I only liked one, but we chose the one we could both agree on. I often have wondered if I had told her to go ahead and choose china on her own and she had chosen the ones with the tiny cup handles, I probably would have complained about those stupid handles every time we used them for the rest of our married life. She, in response, could justifiably say, how was she supposed to know I didn't want tiny cup handles? After all, I said I didn't care! Turns out I really did care more than I realized.

There is one more concept that plays into dealing with issues and that is how will we know an issue is resolved. Obviously, it depends on the issue. Some issues are easy to assess the resolution. For example, what should I have for lunch can be an unresolved issue until I choose the foods that I am about to eat. I ate the tuna sandwich: issue is resolved. Other issues can be more difficult to assess. Let's use the awareness wheel as we assess this situation.

The father was very concerned about his son. The dad was an accomplished athlete and had really wanted his son to follow in his footsteps. However, as the son grew older in age and grew in stature, it became apparent that the son was not interested in athletics. The father worked hard at introducing his son to a wide range of sports activities hoping any one of them might spark some interest. As his son finished high school and went on to college, the father continued to brainstorm new athletic endeavors that his son could try. The son was not interested. Dad was relentless in researching and attempting every new game, sport, athletic endeavor he could find.

Observations thus far:

Dad is an accomplished athlete, very coordinated and wants very much for his son to find a sport that the two might do together. The son has no interest in any sports.

The father is having a difficult time accepting that the issue for his son is over. There will be no sport that he wants to pursue. There is no athletic activity that will peak some interest. The son wants his dad to stop trying to entice him into a sport. The father refuses to take no for an answer. When will the issue be over? Obviously it would come to an end the minute the son agreed to do a sport. Or it would come to an end as soon as the father accepted his son's stance against pursuing physical exercise. But the end will not come easily. Why? Neither the father nor the son is willing to change his behavior to meet the other person's expectation. As long as each one maintains his stance, the issue will be unresolved indefinitely.

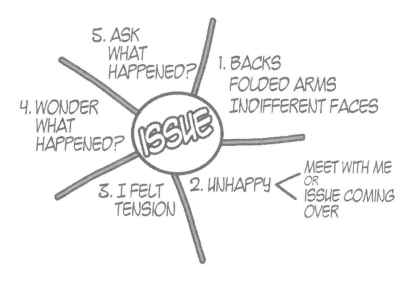

Chapter 11
EXERCISES IN INTERDEPENDENCE

In chapter four, we looked at the process of people growing together in a form of interdependence. Over the years, I have questioned couples concerning what they thought was the ultimate goal of being together. The answers were diverse. Some people, who were influenced by biblical backgrounds, were quick to cite one or several of the texts from the Old Testament wisdom book of Ecclesiastes that has been interpreted, "Two are better than one because they have a good return for their work; if one falls down, his friend can help him up."(Ecclesiastes 4:9) Others cite the second portion of this text (Ecclesiastes 4:11), "Also, if two lie down together, they will keep warm. But how can one keep warm alone?" Still other couples recall the importance of self-preservation. "Though one may be overpowered, two can defend themselves." (Ecclesiastes 4:12a)

For people coming from more carnal backgrounds, their stated goal of being married was sex. For other folks with more familial goals, it was the outcome from sex: having children. In other words, creating and raising a family was the perceived ultimate goal of the union. Every one of these understandings is capable of being true for any two people.

However, I was impressed when I heard a (long since forgotten) speaker tell me that the goal of interdependent relationships was intimacy. It was fascinating to pursue the conversation with people over the years. As I kept track of the conversational suggestions, I discovered there were nine different intimacies that people mentioned they could pursue if they so desired. Each of these intimacies carried with them choices to be made and outcomes that would result. These are not necessarily an exhaustive list, but they are a good place to start. You may want to create and pursue others.

In my second parish I took on the responsibility of teaching the premarital class. We offered the class monthly, and I was able to develop the following list of nine intimacies and provide some questions and exercises for couples to try if they wanted to develop that particular intimacy further. Here are the nine intimacies that were part of my class syllabus. They are listed in a random order – no importance is implied by where an item appears in the list.

Recreational intimacy: this is the ability to share experiences of fun, recreation and/or hobbies together. Finding a common ground that two people can enjoy sharing together. Exercise that I suggested to further this form of togetherness: List two activities you both like doing together. How often do you do them together now? How often would you like to share the activity? When will we next do the event? Be specific in setting a day/time.

Intellectual intimacy: this is being able to share the world of ideas with your partner based on mutual respect. Every idea, no matter how new or different, is given the opportunity to be expressed, discussed, evaluated and considered. Will all ideas ultimately be accepted? No. However, there is no fear in bringing up an idea for consideration and reflection. No judgment is passed on to the person who brings up the idea either. Exercise: When was the last time you sat and talked at length about a book, an issue, a movie, or a topic? Each of you create a list of books, issues, movies, or topics you would like to discuss with your partner. Now, agree on a day and time you will discuss one of the items from each list. When all the items on each list has been exhausted, consider creating a new list and set new times to discuss each.

Work intimacy: sharing common tasks or responsibilities so that the household can function. A married couple befriended me when I was a single student in seminary the first time. Home cooked meals were a delight in their apartment. They shared with me a practice they did every year on the day after their anniversary. They created a list of all the tasks that needed to be done in order for their household to function. Someone has to do laundry, dishes, buy groceries, service the car(s), pay the bills, clean the bathroom, vacuum the floors, etc. Once the list was created, they held their annual draft. She would choose an item off the list, and then he would choose a different item. They took turns choosing tasks until every item was accounted for on the list. They would now be responsible for that task for the next year. Neither of them could assume the other person was going to do the task – they had willingly chosen their items. Did they like their choices? Not always. But if there are only two items left and he or she didn't like either of them, too bad! Choose one and do it. It certainly got away from any sexist assumptions. One year she took on getting the oil changed on the car, and he was responsible for vacuuming. Since neither of them liked paying bills, they agreed they would alternate every year. Work intimacy became a shared part of their interdependence. Exercise: Create a list of tasks that you need to have accomplished for your relationship to continue. Take turns volunteering to be responsible for one item at a time. Be sure to follow through and do the items on your list in a timely fashion. As the year unfolds, be sure to give thanks and affirmation to the other person for following through with the items on his/her list. A benefit of this approach is that one person may not be stuck with an item forever. If, like my friends, a couple chooses to redraft every year, it is quite possible that the list can change from year to year. It is never assumed that the same person has to do the same tasks every year.

Aesthetic intimacy: sharing enjoyment of beauty in any of many forms: music, art, nature, theater. Over the years, I have observed couples who really enjoy spending time together attending arts events. A pastor friend spent several years serving a small church in a very rural community of western Minnesota. In due time, he was issued a new call to a church in the larger metropolitan area of the Twin Cities. The first thing he and his wife did when they moved to the larger city was purchase season tickets to the Minnesota Orchestra and season tickets to the St. Paul Chamber Orchestra. Their years living on the prairie had been very fulfilling in ministry, but they as a couple really missed the opportunities to see and hear classical music. I have known other couples who shared an enjoyment of art and made sure they were always participating in art experiences, even if one partner was enthusiastic about sculpture and the other partner was energized by gardening. Their passion was not only doing the arts personally but also making sure to visit museums and exhibitions every chance they could. Their shared intimacy allowed them to enjoy their aesthetic side together. Exercise: As a couple, each take a turn describing a time in your relationship that you have fond memories. What made that moment so beautiful and/or memorable? Is there a place with particularly important or meaningful aesthetic appeal that you would like to visit with your partner? Where is it? When might the two of you choose to go there?

Emotional intimacy: a place of trust with your partner that allows you to share deep feelings without fear or reservation. These feelings may be on a variety of fronts, not necessarily just about the other person. Emotional intimacy is an important ingredient of any "best friend" relationship. Father John Powell once created lists of feeling words and invited his readers to think of a time he/she had felt each of those feelings. The task wouldn't have seemed so overwhelming except that his list included 207 words! I never dreamed there were that many words to describe emotions. At the end of this section, I will offer you a sample of words he listed. An interesting exercise would be to consider each word and ask yourself if or when you have felt the emotion. Is it a comfortable emotion to feel? Have you ever shared the feeling with others? What additional words would you add to your feeling list?

Accepted, affectionate, afraid, alienated; beautiful, bewildered, brave; cheated, calm, compassionate, confident, confused; dejected, depressed, deprived, domineering; easy going, embarrassed, envious, evasive; fatalistic, fearful, flirtatious, friendly, frustrated; generous, giddy, grateful, guilty; happy, hateful, hostile, humorous; ignored, impatient, inadequate, in control, inferior, inhibited, isolated; judgmental; lonely, lovable, loyal; manipulative, melancholy, misunderstood; needy, narcissistic; optimistic, out of control, overlooked; passionate, peaceful, persecuted, pessimistic, phony, prejudiced, proud; quiet; rejected, religious, remorseful, rewarded; sad, sadistic, secure, seductive, shallow, shy, stubborn, sunshiny; tender, terrified, threatened, tolerant, two-faced; ugly, unappreciated, understanding, unrestrained, uptight; victimized, vindictive, violent; weary, weepy, winner, wishy-washy; youthful.

Commitment intimacy: sharing a common cause with a person. It may be political, religious, service, or athletically oriented. One of the avenues for building we-ness between people is finding causes that two people share in common. I recall a couple who met volunteering at a youth camp. They both enjoyed working with kids and being in the outdoors. When they met at the camp, they already had a shared commitment to working with teens and the environment. It didn't take long for their mutual interests to bring them into proximity. Once there, they had plenty of opportunity to build a relationship that made the most of mutual commitments and interpersonal attraction. An exercise I suggest to couples is to explore what are the commitments that they share in common. That allows them the opportunity to build even greater we-ness having the shared commitments. As you think of your partner (real or imagined for the future), which commitment activities would get you in touch with folks of a similar interest? Spend time there and pursue the relationships that may be discovered.

Communication intimacy: sharing honest, truthful, constructive facts, ideas, and feelings with another person. When we find ourselves in this kind of relationship, there seems to be very little time spent being evasive. These are people you may see every day, and you are comfortable talking honestly with what is going on in your life. These folks are also friends we don't see very often, but when we do get together, we pick up right where we left off. No awkward conversations. Just honestly glad to see you, and here is what I have been up to doing, thinking, and experiencing. An exercise I often recommend is to go through our memory bank and make a list of folks for each decade that fit into this category. Were there any people in my 1 to 10 years; my 11-20 years; my twenties, thirties and as many decades as we have compiled in life. Some folks have reported that they had lots of close communication intimate friends at certain times in their lives but not at other times. The obvious question then becomes what changed? Did the people, the environment, the life circumstances, or locations play a role in the change? Others report that they couldn't think of any close communication friendships in any decade. These folks have the opportunity to reflect on what prevented the intimacy from taking place. Still others can name people in every decade. They obviously know how to make that happen consciously or unconsciously.

Spiritual intimacy: sharing a common moral compass, liturgical tradition, prayer and worship practices, or biblical values in common. People who share this kind of intimacy can spend quality time together with their God (higher power) and people with shared values. In 2014 I had the opportunity to take a study leave from my congregation and spend time traveling in Namibia, West Africa. Our trip included spending a Pentecost Sunday in the city of Swakupmund. As an ordained Lutheran pastor, I was interested in visiting a Lutheran church in the city. It was an amazing experience. I was over 9,000 miles away from my church in Las Vegas, yet I was welcomed as a brother. I was invited to preach to the congregation through an interpreter; I was encouraged to see the congregation wearing the traditional red scarves or ties that is common practice in my church in the United States on Pentecost. As the pastor welcomed me and our delegation, he was very genuine in expressing his warm appreciation for our presence in the service. His only common denominator with us: our spiritual connection through the Lutheran tradition of Christianity. The service was one of the most moving worship experiences I have had outside the United States. Our common faith tradition, our common liturgy, our shared lectionary (using the same texts in Lutheran churches everywhere) enabled total strangers to have an intimate time of worship together. The barriers of not being of the same nationality or not being able to speak the same language did not prevent us from connecting on a spiritual level. Exercise: Think back across your lifetime. Has there been a time when you were part of a spiritual gathering that was deep, inspiring, encouraging, and welcoming? Where did it take place? Who was there? What made that moment so memorable for you?

Sexual intimacy: sharing meaningful sexual expressions. This is probably the intimacy that almost every engaged couple thinks is the ultimate intimacy. Yes, being naked with another person seems very intimate. But I will never forget watching the 1977 movie "Saturday Night Fever" starring John Travolta. There was a scene that took place outside the dance hall. The movie only showed a dark parked car. The audio made it very clear that there were two people engaged in some major physical activity in the back seat. As the groans grew to a crescendo, the male voice says: "What was your name again?" They had supposedly just performed the most intimate act two people can share, yet he had not bothered to learn his partner's name! Being naked, or exposed, is not necessarily intimacy.

Regarding sexual expression, I had a professor once tell our class that there is a four letter word for great sex (drum roll) TALK. Her suggestion was that for the best results in giving and receiving physical pleasure, talk about what you find enjoyable and let your partner tell you what he/she enjoys. Most people use the Christopher Columbus method, she said. Search and land and hope you were correct! A better approach might be to talk about the following questions: What do I like in foreplay? Which expressions will we use to express ourselves? When do we want to express ourselves sexually? Where is it appropriate to express our sexual interests? How do we say "No" for now? The answers to these questions can go a long way to making the meaning of the physical intimacy of sexual expressions more fulfilling.

Bibliography

Chapter One

Harris, Thomas A. *I'm Ok—You're Ok* Harper & Row, New York 1967, 1968, 1969

Chapter Two

Miller, Nunnally, Wackman *Talking and Listening Together* Interpersonal Communications Programs, Inc. Littleton, CO. 1991

Chapter Three

Karpman, Stephen B. *A Game Free Life* Drama Triangle Publications, San Francisco, 2011

Chapter Six

Swenson, Richard, A. *Margin* Navpress Colorado Springs, CO 1992

Chapter Seven

Powell, John *Why Am I Afraid to Tell You Who I Am?*

Argus Communications, Niles, Il 1969

Chapter Eleven

Concordia Self-Study Bible, New International Version

Concordia Publishing House, St. Louis, Mo 1986

ABOUT THE AUTHOR

Dr. Mark Wickstrom has spent his entire career leading, learning about and helping people. As a pastor Mark has served in three large congregations and he has had the opportunity to counsel with men and women, boys and girls of all ages. He has gained insights on the workings of a wide range of relationships. Mark is a visual learner and he has always been intrigued with how to use diagrams to make abstract situations or complex circumstances more understandable. Mark and his wife Kristi successfully launched all four of their children and currently live in Las Vegas, Nevada.

Other Books by Dr. Mark Wickstrom

Gospel of Grace, Tools for Building a Positive
Understanding of the Bible

Beaver's Pond Press Edina, MN, 2008, 2012

Workbook for Gospel of Grace,

MDW Press, Las Vegas, NV, 2010

James Book of Faith Series

Augsburg Fortress, Minneapolis, MN, 2010

67721519R00076

Made in the USA
Charleston, SC
20 February 2017